The Stress Less Mind

Daily Survival Guide to staying on top of **Your Life**

By Georgia Foster

Internationally Renowned Hypnotherapist

Georgia Foster asserts the moral right to be identified as the author and publisher of this work

Proofread by Freya Martin, www.ultimateproof.co.uk

Music composed by Nick Crofts

CD Recording: Lloyd Dukes, www.bushstudios.co.uk

CD Duplication: www.soundrecordingtechnology.co.uk

Design and typeset by Fever Design, www.fever-design.co.uk

Published by Georgia Foster Publishing
www.georgiafoster.com

ISBN: 978-0-9560132-3-1

A catalogue record for this book is available from the British Library

Printed in Great Britain by the MPG Books Group,
Bodmin and King's Lynn

About the Author

Georgia Foster has been working as a Clinical Hypnotherapist and Voice Dialogue Trainer since 1995 in London, United Kingdom. Originally from Melbourne, Australia, her personal experience with low self-esteem and food issues led to years of self-exploration to find answers.

This book represents her successful work with thousands of people.

Other books by Georgia Foster:
Free To Be
Releasing the Writer's Block
The 4 Secrets of Amazing Sex (co-authored with Beverley Anne Foster)
The Weight Less Mind™
The Drink Less Mind

Acknowledgements

My biggest thanks are to my beautiful parents who are the most amazing, unconditional, loving people a daughter could ask for. My funny and clever sister Virginia, thank you for your wisdom and laughter.

My mum Beverley Anne, once again you have worked tirelessly on editing this book. I can't thank you enough!

Thanks to Sue Blake, my UK publicist, who has believed in me right from the start as well as my tirelessly patient assistant, Janice.

I would also like to say thanks to Di Rolle, my publicist in Australia, who jumps in when I have a trip home to help my book and workshop sales. You are a star Di!

I am welcoming on board with this book, Katie Romero-Stellar and John Stellar, from Stellar Communications, for your faith in me as a new client. I am so looking forward to our journey ahead together.

Thanks to Steve Verity from Fever Design for his consistent support with my new ideas and deadlines.

To Suzy Greaves and Viv Alves, my new business partners in The Big Life Events Company. It's been wonderful to have like-minded people to start an amazing business together.

Thank you to all of my clients, book readers and workshop participants who have helped build my business by your word of mouth and amazing results.

Contents

Chapter 1
Introduction

The
Stress
Less
Mind

Introduction

Stress is an experience that we can all resonate with at different times of our lives, for it is a part of life. Stress is a sign that something is not right. We may not necessarily read the signs nor hear them, but, nonetheless, stress is the major player in emotional and physical illnesses.

Through the years, all over the world, men and women who have read my previous books, attended workshops or seen me privately at my clinic have all been searching. Their search I soon discovered was for how they could learn to train their mind so that they could cope better with their own stress or the stress of another person which then indirectly created stress within them. Let me explain this conundrum, a stressed person can create stress in the people who surround them be they wife, husband, CEO or fellow worker. The aim of people seeking my help is to enable their mind to cope with the impact of stress in their lives.

I could go on forever about the thousands of people who have read my books, attended workshops or seen me privately. Irrespective of their ailment or reason for seeing me, they all had a common goal. They wanted to know how to train their mind to cope better with life.

Getting Out of the Stress Rut

The Stress Less Mind is a self-help book with a difference. Contained inside the back cover is a unique CD which gives you an opportunity to break the patterns of thoughts that trigger stress. Through listening to *The Stress Less Mind* CD you will be able to create new ways of responding when you find yourself under stress. You will discover a renewed sense of confidence and freedom so that you will be better able to cope with stress and stressful situations. *The Stress Less Mind* CD will help you reconnect with the inner relaxed and confident you, so you will be more adept at handling stress.

I am not suggesting that once you read *The Stress Less Mind* and listen to the accompanying CD that you will be the happiest person on this earth, rather that the book and CD will help you understand how to create within you an emotional mechanism so you will be able to recognize the signs of stress. Through re-training your mind you will learn and understand how not to go there as frequently or as deeply. This way you will learn new ways of responding to the different aspects of your life so that you discover self-worth, a sense of direction and faith about you in your present situation and your future.

The Hamster Stress Wheel

The signs of stress are many and varied. Perhaps you already know what stress signals lie within you and yet, even though you are aware of these signs you cannot get off the Hamster Stress Wheel. The Hamster Stress Wheel keeps turning and churning inside you because you do not know how to press the stop button and get off. When you do not know how to get off the Hamster Stress Wheel you just keep going around and around because you feel there is no other solution but to keep going. Or you may be so used to feeling stressed that it feels normal to you and so you keep churning away on the Hamster Stress Wheel without realizing the detrimental effect on your health and wellbeing as well as on your ability to function positively in life.

The more you ride the Hamster Stress Wheel the more you are affirming that life is stressful and that you feel unable to relax your mind and take time out for you. Stress helps to create a variety of physical symptoms which can lead to illness.

The Stress Less Mind explains why stress is the number one emotional disease in the western world and how it can lead to the suffocation of belief in your own ability to get the best out of life. How you interpret your stress and react to it depends on one thing – how you think and feel about you!

Acknowledging stress can be difficult for many of us because we all like to think we can cope with anything that comes our way. Many of us feel too embarrassed to admit that we are stressed because we feel we may lose our job, or the respect of our colleagues, or that people will see us as being weak or useless.

There are so many varied signs of stress. Perhaps you can identify what they are within yourself, even though you know you still can't get off the Hamster Stress Wheel to deal with them because there doesn't seem to be any other solution except to just keep going. Or perhaps you don't recognize the signs of stress simply because you are so used to feeling stressed that it just seems to be a normal way of living.

Perhaps it could also be that you are showing some serious signs of stress that have created an illness, and you have been advised that you have to change your lifestyle because stress is literally killing you!

The following list contains just 12 of the many signs of stress.

- repetitive negative thoughts
- self-doubt
- anxiety and fear
- paranoia
- low self-esteem
- insomnia or sleeping too much
- weight loss or weight gain
- wanting to retreat from the world
- excessive drinking
- excessive smoking
- depression
- suicidal thoughts

You are stressed for a reason. It is your mind telling you that you are not in a good place in life either emotionally or physically. Stress is an alarm bell that will keep ringing within you until it is ultimately heard. If it isn't, then serious emotional and physical consequences will occur.

Negative Thinking, Anxiety and Fear

Many people assume that migraines and insomnia are related to stress, which the are. However, the most common stress symptoms are, in fact, the result of anxiety, negative thinking and fear.

The Stress Less Mind is about training your mind to alleviate these negative states of mind, and guess what happens when you do this? You cope better, you feel better and things don't get to you as much as they used to. You notice that you CAN do it rather than you can't. It becomes clear that change is possible because you feel calmer and more confident to make the changes that are truly right for you.

You may be reading this and thinking, "Yeah, right, Georgia, easy for you to say when you don't have three kids to feed, a husband who is out of work and a mountain of bills to pay." However, I do get your point because I have had some amazingly stressful moments in my life. The difference is that now, when things are going down that stress road, I know the signs and how to deal with them by changing my thinking.

We are all open to negative thinking and we are also open to difficult situations that make us feel vulnerable.

Glass Half Full or Half Empty?

A client asked me if I could help him change a lifetime of negative thinking so that the glass was half full rather than half empty. I smiled and said of course, but I asked him to do one thing first. That was to have the courage to see if his glass of life was half full then he might just have to be happy.

This may seem a strange thing to have told my client but it is true. Many of my clients, like a lot of people, have created the habit of always thinking the worst and then this simply becomes their usual way of thinking. Not deliberately of course, but as a way of protecting themselves from emotional harm or upset.

That is the irony of the mind. It thinks planning for the worst case scenario prepares you like a good Girl Guide or Boy Scout. However, it then sets you up for always expecting the worst outcome, which makes you more stressed and anxious.

So many of my clients believe that if they think negatively first then at least they won't be disappointed and let down. They have literally trained themselves to assume the worst will happen so, when it does, they are fully prepared for it. How stressful is that? Actually, it is a very common belief. Generation after generation of indoctrination has led us into this way of thinking so we believe that when the glass is half empty we won't get let down by life.

If you think this applies to you then your mind is regularly thinking negatively and this will be causing you undue stress and anxiety about your life that is completely unnecessary.

It is impossible to feel calm and in control of your life if you are constantly worrying about what might happen, or trying to predict the future. These "crystal ball" moments of thinking make you fear your future.

The Stress Less Mind is going to literally train your mind to feel calm and confident. You will see life as a trusting experience, full of lots of good things to look forward to in your future.

Emotional Habits

The unconscious mind is where all the emotional experiences of life are stored. Just like a library, we use it every day and every night as a reference for how we assume we are meant to deal with our life.

You may notice that after an unusually stressful day, you reach for that extra large glass of wine, or that you eat too much, or that you feel really tense and anxious and just can't relax. You may toss and turn through the night and wake feeling exhausted in the morning, dreading the next day because you are so tired and feeling less able to cope than the day before. You may then realize that all of a sudden you have put on 40 pounds, or that you can't remember the last time you didn't take a sleeping tablet before bed, or that you don't want to socialize because you feel too drained to deal with other people.

You may not notice that this is your pattern of behavior. You feel stressed, and then you become edgy, a little bit snappy and angry with other people. You start to repeat these coping strategies, such as drinking excess alcohol, using sleeping tablets or smoking 60 cigarettes a day to help you cope with your life.

These sorts of responses are what I call your "unconscious stress management tools." You may think consciously, "Why would I want to sabotage my health and wellbeing by resorting to this excessive behavior?" but your unconscious mind has literally learned that this is how you cope.

The unconscious mind is where all your emotional habits are stored and, when you feel stressed, it will, in a millisecond, scan your mind asking itself, "When did I last feel like this and how did I make myself feel better?" If it was thinking the worst case scenario, such as: "Am I going to lose my job?" then your mind will recreate these feelings of panic and you will want to run away. This is called stress! When you feel the need to escape from your life you may hear yourself say, "I can't cope. What is wrong with me?" You then start to question who you are and notice that you don't like yourself as much and that everything is just plain hard work.

Exhaustion sets in and everything becomes too difficult to deal with. Then moments that used to be manageable become unmanageable and everything becomes completely out of proportion.

Positive and Negative Thinking

It may seem bizarre to some but the mind doesn't know the difference between positive and negative. It doesn't understand that being calm is better than feeling anxious. It doesn't know that feeling safe is better for you than feeling scared. The library of your unconscious mind will use past experiences as your learned response, whether you consciously want to or not!

If you deal with stress by negative thinking, this does not support you and instead causes you more stress. Then your mind will automatically assume that this is the correct response because it is learned information your unconscious mind draws from.

If you say to yourself, "I'm feeling stressed" or "I'm feeling scared," your mind will automatically resort to its last response, which may not necessarily be helpful and may in fact hinder your health and wellbeing.

The Stress Less Mind and the accompanying CD guides your mind on how to learn new responses that support you to feel good about yourself, even in the eye of the very stressful storm of life!

Moving On From the Past

The greatest challenge for many people who come to see me is that they don't know how to learn new coping strategies. They ask me, "Why am I continually repeating these ridiculous behaviors and why am I feeling so out of control?"

This is where the unconscious mind can appear to be the problem. This frustrating inability to cope better or feel better makes you feel down about yourself and low self-esteem can set in, and this is often followed by depression.

Is it any surprise that if your past represents difficult moments such as rejection, hurt, fear, anxiety and out-of-control feelings due to stressful life experiences, your mind will have educated itself that feeling stressed is the normal response?

Habitual stressful mind statements include: "You're not coping." "Everybody is better and more clever than you." "The reason you are in this situation is because you don't have the ability to get out of it. This is your life." Of course, there may be times in your life when things have been great, but underpinning these moments will be a feeling of, "Yeah, but for how long?" Does this sound familiar?

The unconscious mind is a powerful tool that can work against any hopes or dreams. If you feel as if life has thrown difficult moments in your way, then after a period of time, your unconscious mind thinks this is how your life is meant to be – difficult!

The truth is we all have the ability to make healthy changes in our lives but we need the help of the unconscious mind. This part of the mind needs to learn new coping mechanisms that represent your present and your future rather than your learned past responses.

People ask me how can this be possible? Believe me it is extremely possible. Listening to the accompanying CD regularly will help it become a reality for you, because learning new positive ways of reacting and responding to your life just takes practice.

A therapist friend once said to me that the definition of insanity is doing the same thing over and over again, knowing that it is not getting you anywhere. Most of our stress management tools don't get us anywhere either. We keep repeating the same negative behaviors, praying that maybe one day these behaviors might change. They won't change unless you change your responses.

By creating new references in your unconscious mind's library, you are giving your mind an opportunity to see and feel things from a healthier perspective. In the following chapters you are going to learn how to do this easily, effortlessly and naturally with the support of *The Stress Less Mind* CD.

If, at present, your mind is using habitual learned reactionary responses it is time to move on from these.

Your Bodily Functions

The unconscious mind is where all the bodily functions are stored. This part of the mind produces certain stress chemicals when you experience fear or anxiety. These chemicals trigger real physical pain such as panic attacks, anxiety, heart palpitations, shortness of breath, sweating and sometimes a feeling of being frozen.

When you feel confident, your body responds with positive chemicals – endorphins and the knock-on effect is that your physical body becomes more relaxed and everything becomes just that little bit easier to deal with.

Your mind has to make a choice - either feel stressed and anxious, or calm and confident. It cannot produce stress chemicals and endorphins at the same time. Without being aware of it, your unconscious mind has trained itself to over-produce stress chemicals as the response to life. So, this is the good news. If your mind has, over a period of time, educated itself to think stressful thoughts which produce stress chemicals, it can learn how to produce the exact opposite.

While listening to *The Stress Less Mind* CD your mind is learning how to create these endorphins which will allow you to feel calmer, clearer and more positive about you. It does take practice, but then everything does. Your unconscious mind has practiced how to experience stress as the normal response to your life and now all it needs to do is simply learn the opposite so that it knows how to feel better about you.

The New Positive School of Emotional Learning

The following chapters will take you to a place where you will be able to resonate with why you feel stressed and how to move on from it. This new learning center of emotional health and wellbeing already exists within you; it just needs to be given the opportunity to flourish.

As I previously mentioned, and I feel it is important to repeat, the unconscious mind is where all your emotional and physical habits are stored, so it makes sense for you to go to that part of the mind to learn how to respond differently. If you can imagine the word "hypnosis" is like attending a new school, this will be a school where you will enjoy learning new ways of thinking and responding. If your mind has trained itself through life experiences to think that you are less worthy than others, or perhaps that everything is too hard or difficult to deal with, over a period of time, regardless of the truth, it will consider these negative thoughts to be the truth. It is now time to change this negative thinking into positive thinking and enjoy life.

All you need is 25 minutes a day to listen to *The Stress Less Mind* CD while you are sitting or lying somewhere comfortable. You must be stationary throughout listening to the CD. If you need to wake at any time, you can do so by simply opening your eyes.

Don't worry if you fall asleep, it won't make any difference. You may notice, depending on what time of day or night it is, that sometimes you will be more awake than at others. The good news is that even while you are sleeping you will be absorbing all of these positive life changes which you have the right to enjoy.

The School of Hypnosis

The word "hypnosis" is often incorrectly associated with losing control, that you won't be in control of your thoughts or actions but, in fact, the exact opposite is true. During the hypnotic state you are more intuitive than you are in the conscious state. It is a heightened state of mind where you are able to learn at a much faster rate.

In order for you to go to sleep at night you have to go through the hypnotic state. It is that half-asleep/half-awake experience before you fall asleep, and just before you wake in the morning you go through the same experience. This is when you are in the hypnotic state. While listening to *The Stress Less Mind* CD you will find yourself drifting in and out of awareness. You may notice that at certain times you will be less aware of what you are listening to, while at other times you will be very aware. There is no right or wrong way to experience hypnosis; however, you will notice after a while, as you become used to the experience, that you look forward to taking this time out for yourself.

We very rarely take time out for ourselves. This is one of the major problems of our everyday fraught lives – we don't feel we have enough time. The CD contained within *The Stress Less Mind* book will educate you to be more relaxed, less stressed and more confident. If you truly feel you don't have time to listen to it, then put it on as you go to sleep at night. If you do fall asleep, the good news is that the information is still being absorbed. Your unconscious mind is open 24 hours a day even while you sleep, so just trust that the information is being stored as your new coping strategy.

The more your mind hears and feels these words, the more it is learning that this is your positive coping strategy. It is the positive way to deal with whatever comes your way, irrespective of your past.

Before you start to listen to the CD, I would like to explain how it works. A lot of people have many misconceptions about what hypnosis feels like. Here are some common questions and answers regarding the CD and hypnosis.

Q. Will I fall asleep?
A. Some people do fall asleep. This will not change the results of the self-hypnosis. Remember, the information is still going into your mind. The unconscious mind is open to receive and store information 24 hours a day. It is not for you to disagree, it is a fact.

Q. When is the best time to listen to the CD?
A. The best time is before you go to sleep, but often some of my clients do not want their partners to know what they are listening to. If this applies to you, then perhaps listen to your CD

during lunch time, somewhere safe, or in a room or office where you know you will not be disturbed. Some people love waking up and listening to the CD – they feel that it sets them up for the day.

Q. If I am interrupted when listening to the CD, does it mean it hasn't worked?
A. No, not at all. It just means that you haven't completed the CD track, so maybe try it again later.

Q. Can other people listen to the CD?
A. No, tell them to go and buy their own book! You made the effort, you spent the money, and they can too if they are serious about it! It is important for you to become healthily selfish and take time out for you.

Q. If my mind is busy, is it still working?
A. Yes, absolutely. It doesn't make any difference. You will, on some level, be absorbing the information. It will also help you to relax and you should look forward to this down-time/recharge-time.

Q. If I move around while lying or sitting down will it bring me out of hypnosis?
A. No, just move around if you need to during the CD. A lot of people, when they are relaxed, recognize how much tension they hold in their body, so any adjustments are beneficial. If you want to cough, scratch or sneeze it will not make any difference.

A Little Tip

The moments you are feeling stressed are the exact times you need to schedule in time to listen to the CD. You may say to yourself that you don't have time, but it will actually give you more real clock time because taking time out for 25 minutes will, in fact, be rejuvenating your body as well as your mind. The lovely "domino effect" means that your mind will become clearer, you will have more energy and, as life will be in a much more positive perspective, you will cope better.

Something to Think About

- You have the right to feel good about yourself.
- You are now starting to build new important coping tools for your mind that are supporting you rather than working against you.
- Your mind understands now that by listening to the CD you are on your way to dealing much more healthily and confidently with life.

So let's now explore the amazing mind you have from the perspective of a Stress Less Mind.

Over the next few chapters you will begin to explore some amazing aspects of your emotional life and how you have the ability to change your thinking so you are less stressed.

Chapter 2
Inner Dialogue

Inner Dialogue

Throughout my years of being a therapist the predominant treatment involved in the success of my work comes from the powerful theory that I call "Inner Dialogue."

You may not recognize it consciously, but our mind is constantly chattering to itself most of the time. For some people it is mainly positive chatter, but for others the chatter is full of negative statements that hold the individual to emotional ransom.

Below is a short list to help you identify some negative self-talk.

What Does Negative Self-Talk Sound Like?

- You've bought this book and you think it is going to be a miracle cure. Yeah right!
- Everybody else copes better than you.
- You're hopeless, what makes you think you have the ability to feel better?
- You are a bad person. People are just being kind. They don't really like you.
- Feeling good doesn't last long, so what is the point of going there?
- If people really knew me they wouldn't like me.
- I am a fake. I am going to get caught out one day that I am actually not that nice.

Situations Beyond Your Control

Patricia came to see me because she was feeling completely stressed and lost in her life. She had been made redundant twice due to situations beyond her control. Both companies she worked for got caught up in over-capitalizing and when the industry hit the recession Patricia became a victim of it.

Patricia clearly had a good work history and was more than capable of climbing the corporate ladder that she so wished to do and yet the woman who came to see me was a lifeless, tearful, fearful and anxiety-ridden human being.

These two job situations were completely beyond Patricia's control and the stress she had been placed under financially and emotionally was creating anxiety, low self-worth and negative thinking. By the time Patricia came to see me she had decided that she didn't want to go back into the computer industry that she had once enjoyed. The money she had been given from both redundancies had run out and she was living off her credit cards.

Some of her so-called friends had abandoned her (which often happens) and Patricia felt there was no point in doing anything because she was too tired and didn't have the energy to go out there again, only to be rejected.

I asked Patricia if she was aware of how negatively she was talking to herself. She looked bemused. I smiled as this is often the look I get.

We are always talking to ourselves, negatively or positively. For those who suffer from regular stress there will be a negative conversation going on in their head. I asked Patricia if she heard statements within her own mind that reflected the following: "Everybody thinks you are a loser," "Other people keep their jobs, why can't you?" "No point in trying to get another job, you will just lose it," "You can get away with being made redundant once but not twice."

Radio Crazy Syndrome

Patricia was flabbergasted. She asked me, "How did you know that was what I was thinking?" I answered, "It's easy, you have what I refer to as Radio Crazy Syndrome."

If you are suffering from stress it's guaranteed that the conversations in your head are so negatively charged that you feel as if you are literally going mad. Radio Crazy Syndrome is, unfortunately, for many of us a way of life. How you talk to yourself is actually destroying any hopes or dreams of moving out of the stressful situation because your negative Inner Dialogue is holding you in jail. You are being kept a prisoner and so cannot move on to learn new coping strategies.

Patricia's redundancy was one of those unfortunate situations over which she had no control. Twice she had suffered life-shattering moments related to her work. Patricia's Radio Crazy statements ran around in her mind constantly. Patricia started to believe these negative statements. She began to believe that she must be an awful person and that nobody wanted to employ her. Patricia's stress levels were extremely high at this point as a result of her anxiety and fear, which were deepening her low self-worth.

I don't know anybody who suffers from stress who doesn't have Radio Crazy Syndrome because this is the catalyst to creating and maintaining negative thinking.

The truth is we all suffer from Radio Crazy conversations, some of us more than others and at certain times in our lives it will be stronger than at other times. The trick is to recognize what triggers your Radio Crazy conversations and the signals that it sends you so that you don't have to fall back into the stress trap like before.

Self-Fulfilling Prophecy

The unconscious mind is a powerful tool. It stores all of the emotional experiences we have had, both positive and negative. If you have experienced any form of highly negatively charged moments, such as rejection, abuse or criticism then your unconscious mind may have stored them without you being aware of it. And then over a period of time, your unconscious mind will assume that this is what you deserve and will give you continued negative statement feedback to affirm that this is how your life is meant to be.

This protective mechanism is like a self-fulfilling prophecy. The more your mind thinks something is normal, whether positive or negative, then the more it will affirm this, simply because your Radio Crazy continues to confirm this.

The Cave Man Days

The Radio Crazy Syndrome stems from a voice that was created originally to protect us early in life against any on coming, potentially stressful moments. It is the classic "fight or flight" syndrome that is often referred to in life as fear and anxiety. Originally, back in the cave man days, the mind would sense a bear coming and make a quick decision to stay and fight or to run away from the situation.

Life has changed since then; however, the bear is still there deep within each of us. All that has happened is that it has been redefined in our modern world as the general stresses we all encounter in every day life.

The Inner Critic

The Inner Critic is the name of the part that underpins the Radio Crazy Syndrome. It is a real voice that is designed solely to protect you against vulnerability. Its purpose is to prepare you and warn you of what might happen, just in case it does. So it sets about planning the worst case scenarios in your mind, just in case they happen, which causes stress and anxiety within you. It is the Inner Critic voice that stores in your unconscious mind all the negative experiences that you have had in your life. It is very good at reminding you of these negative moments at any given time should you choose to listen to it. This is the major problem of people who are stressed; they listen to the Inner Critic constantly without being aware of it and it becomes so strong that they believe its opinions to be true.

The irony of the Inner Critic is that it thinks if it keeps reminding you of all the negative experiences in your life then you will be prepared for them. The result is, in fact, that you keep affirming your perceived failures.

The Big, Black Hole

The Inner Critic can be demonic in some people and it is the part of us that destroys through sabotaging any hopes or dreams. If you have a demonic Inner Critic it voices itself when you decide you want to feel better about yourself. It will then begin to constantly remind you of past, negative life experiences which brings you back into the same negative, anxious state. Like a big, black hole the Inner Critic drags you back into the abyss of negative thoughts and feelings of loss, fear, self-doubt and anger.

This big, black hole can deepen for some people simply because the voice of their Inner Critic is so strong that it feels much too scary for them to actually think of being anything else other than negative. Negativity for these people has become the learned behavior.

The Irony of the Inner Critic

This is the irony of the Inner Critic. The more negatively it voices itself, the more it thinks it is protecting you against the big bear that might be around the corner. The power of this fear-based conversation will suppress any hopes or dreams that may trickle into your life because the Inner Critic thinks it is unsafe to be positive. It makes statements such as: "Everybody is better, more clever, slimmer, healthier, smarter and kinder than you. Who do you think you are?"

If you are regularly stressed, even a twinkling of remembered positive moments in your past often will not be enough to ignite the desire and energy to feel better, rather than stressed. This is because your Inner Critic has drummed into your mind that you are coping even though you are stressed. It keeps repeating that everybody else is better than you, filling your mind with Radio Crazy conversations.

These conversations don't just stay in the mind; they rush madly into every living cell in your body, producing anxiety-based chemicals that make your heart race, skin sweat and your breath cycle shorten, which then creates panicked feelings.

Stress Can Be the Stepping Stone to Depression

The knock-on effect of these feelings then creates an emotionally conditioned response within you that is supported by the Inner Critic's voice. It says, "See, I told you thinking positively is unsafe. Why don't you just stay here in the state of depression where you know your place?"

Time and time again I see clients who have fallen into the same trap – the trap of being overstressed which creates burn out and often depression. I am not suggesting that every stressful situation may be easy to get out of, but if you continually listen to your Inner Critic for long enough, then you will believe that there is no way out of the situation instead of thinking of positive alternatives, and so the negative vicious cycle goes on.

Drinking Your Inner Critic Away

There are a few ways of suppressing the Inner Critic when it gets too much. The most common way is by consuming alcohol and sometimes lots of it!

The alcohol hides the Inner Critic. In fact, this could become one of the ways in which you run away from stressful situations and your Inner Critic on a regular basis. If this is the case you may feel you are alcohol dependent. The good news is that it is less to do with the alcohol and more to do with the feelings you get from drinking.

Alcohol is a great way to get that instant fix of calm or social or sexual confidence, and can block stressful thoughts and feelings to lift your spirits for a bit. However, unfortunately, it also means that you are not dealing with the real issue of why you need the alcohol to make yourself feel better in the first place.

You have to respect that your Inner Critic is a part of you, so there are very few places you can run and hide and, for many, alcohol will be the answer for that moment in time. However, in the morning it is a different story when you wake up feeling a little hung-over and then have a massive Inner Critic attack as it says something like, "Why did you drink so much last night?" "Who do you think you are?" "You really embarrassed yourself last night." "Everybody thinks you're a drunk." This Inner Critic talk triggers anxiety, booze blues and a sense of lower self-worth, and the vicious cycle happens all over again with the desire to drink so you can run away from the Inner Critic.

If your Radio Crazy is overwhelming you then having a glass or two or three or more will dampen the negativity and anxiety that the Inner Critic creates. If you are using alcohol to run away from your negative self-talk then you may wish to purchase my book, *The Drink Less Mind*. This book is a wonderful way to reduce alcohol consumption as well as build self-esteem and better coping strategies.

The Difficult Moments

If you believe your Inner Critic's negative propaganda, you will stay and live more in the state of stress than live in the state of calm. It's a simple equation; stressful thinking multiplied by more stressful thinking creates a stressful response. The more you feel stressed by negative self-talk the more you believe it to be true.

This is not because you consciously want to be stressed, but rather the unconscious mind scans your past method of coping with difficult aspects of your life and sees panic, fear and self-doubt as the answer. It's like going to the library of your life and looking up "Difficult Moments" and seeing "Negative Thinking" as the answer. It's not actually a choice for some, it is simply automatic.

The following are examples of the types of Inner Critic comments that I hear from my clients:

- I feel I am not coping well with my life.
- I can't find the strength to change jobs.
- Everybody else seems to cope better with their lives.
- I know I need to lose weight but I just can't find the motivation.
- I am angry at the world.
- Life is unfair.
- Nothing ever seems to go right in my life.
- What's the point in trying to improve my life, it never lasts anyway.
- I'm not good enough.
- I'm a hopeless case.
- If people really knew me they wouldn't like me.

Does This Sound Familiar?

I could write a whole book on these comments alone, for these are just some of the things that most clients say when we start to work together. To the outside world we all appear differently from how we see ourselves in our own minds and this, fundamentally, is one of the reasons why people over-drink, overeat, smoke too much, take drugs, or sleep too much, plus many more abusive situations. We do it to forget about ourselves and our problems.

So let's check your Inner Critic out by answering the following questionnaire, so you can understand how powerful it is when it comes to creating more unnecessary stress than there should be in your life.

Rating Your Inner Critic

To be rated by: Rarely (1) About Average (3) Frequently (5). Add up your scores at the end and look at the key below for your personal Inner Critic score.

Questions	1/3/5
1. I wake in the night worried about what I didn't achieve yesterday.	
2. I regularly panic about what the future holds.	
3. I feel the glass is half empty rather than half full.	
4. When I'm in company I worry what they are thinking of me.	
5. I procrastinate on a regular basis.	
6. I am always putting myself down.	
7. I feel anxious about making the right decisions.	
8. My sleep is erratic because I am so stressed.	
9. I don't like delegating because people let you down.	
10. I don't think I cope as well as other people.	
11. I don't feel I have the resources to like myself.	
12. I feel I am faking my life.	
13. If people really knew me they wouldn't like me.	
14. I feel vulnerable around people who I think are better than me.	
15. I get angry with myself because I feel I can't move on.	
16. I question my decisions after they have been made and worry whether I have done the right thing.	
17. When I say "No" I feel guilty.	
18. When I take a questionnaire like this, I'm sure that everyone else will do better than me.	
19. I avoid taking risks if I can help it.	
20. When I think about all the things I should have done, I feel I have wasted my life.	

Key to the strength of your Inner Critic:

25-44: Weak

Congratulations, your Inner Critic is well in check. Your self-esteem is high. You have a healthy balance to life and cope with the ups and downs well.

44-74: Medium

Your Inner Critic is strong in certain areas of your life. Usually this means that you are confident in perhaps your personal life and maybe not so confident in your professional life or vice versa. You need to start combating any negative statements with positive ones by writing down what your Inner Critic is saying and then writing down the opposite and saying it positively each time after your Inner Critic speaks to you.

75-plus: Strong

Your Inner Critic plays havoc with your emotional wellbeing and often causes overpowering guilt and unnecessary bouts of low self-worth. Know that you are making an effort to improve your relationship with yourself by reading this book, irrespective of what happened yesterday or what may happen tomorrow.

Avoidance of Life

This is an extract from *The Drink Less Mind* book. It is about a client called John who I feel will resonate with you.

John came to see me a few years ago when at the time he was the CEO of an insurance company. He had worked his way up to this level during his 20 years with the same firm. John explained that he was worried that he wasn't good at his job. I asked him why he thought that and he replied, "I am very embarrassed to say this but I don't work hard, in fact I don't work hard at all. I earn US$500,000 a year plus bonus and I can honestly say I don't deserve this income. In fact, I don't deserve this job. I feel like I am faking it. I feel at any moment I'm going to be found out and they are going to sack me. It's almost like I want to sabotage myself all the time. I tell my assistant that I am out for a business lunch but I go out for hours, buy a newspaper and drink a couple of glasses of wine where no-one can find me. It's terrible but I can't help myself."

John's high level of anxiety was of great concern and it was as clear as day to me that he had a powerful Inner Critic. John's Inner Critic was his strongest voice. And it criticized and berated him in two different ways. The first way it did this was to nag him incessantly at work, telling him that he was inadequate for his position as CEO which in reality was far from the truth. The second way the Inner Critic operated in John's life was to criticize him when he took needed time out for a lunch break because he was anxious and emotionally exhausted. This is when his Inner Critic stepped in yet again and drove him to drink. In other words, John's Inner Critic made him feel overridden with guilt for taking time out to rest and enjoy a glass of wine, and as a result he tried to silence this nagging voice through over-drinking. John's Inner Critic held a tight grip on him and because of this, every time he tried to move out of his Inner Critic voice it consolidated its powerful position even more.

By the time John came to see me, his memory bank was stored with failure. Every way he looked at his life John felt he had failed and was a fake. His Inner Critic nagged him incessantly, telling him: "You aren't educated enough to be in this work." "Everybody else is more clever, better and more appropriate to be CEO than you." "Who do you think you are, earning all this money? It's ridiculous."

Then he felt he had failed when he took time out from work and it turned into running away and over-drinking. John rarely questioned his Inner Critic; instead he listened to it and believed what it said to be true. In other words, he bought into his Inner Critic's propaganda. John was being suffocated and prevented from enjoying his success through not being aware of his own Inner Dialogue. Every extra glass of wine he consumed was a way of drowning out the sound of his Inner Critic.

The Inner Critic's Development

The Inner Critic part has a personality trait that judges and criticizes you. However, it is also the part that was actually created to protect you and keep you safe. And yet, through a lifetime of different experiences, the Inner Critic has trained itself to work against you not for you, and this is why it undermines your self-confidence and ability. For the Inner Critic thinks if it can get in first and get you to listen to what it says then it will prepare you for the worst case scenario, just in case it happens. We all have an Inner Critic, but how we interpret its conversations within our self depends on the strength of our other inner voices/parts, which you will meet in the following chapters. It would be safe for me to say that during my many years of being a therapist, I have heard pretty much every Inner Critic comment made from people from all walks of life.

John's relationship with himself was managed by the Inner Critic and it held him to emotional ransom. The truth is, John is good at his work. Nobody can get away with being bad at their work for 20 years without being found out on some level. The fact is that John's Inner Critic was so powerful that it did two things: it caused him to run away and drink to avoid the anxiety of work, while at the same time he actually worked twice as hard to prove he was good at his job. This was why he was a well-respected CEO. John's Inner Critic had developed in childhood and it held its position of power in his adult life through fear. The Inner Critic feared that if John's self-belief increased, it would lose its stranglehold. Through our sessions and by listening to the CD, John gradually learned how to release his powerful negative Inner Critic voice and feel the energy of calming endorphins so that he was able to relax a little bit more and see the truth – that he was good at what he did. Much to John's surprise and relief, he found that his co-workers responded positively as he became happier and more relaxed. And as this happened, John's confidence grew, his anxiety levels dropped and his habit of running away at lunch time or in the afternoon to consume a few drinks was no longer a part of his life.

Silent but Violent

When you purchased *The Stress Less Mind* you did so because something stirred within you. Perhaps it is a concern about how you are going to cope with ongoing stresses or perhaps you are feeling trapped in your life. There are a multitude of reasons why people are stressed.

Believe me that not one person really knows what another person is thinking at any given time, otherwise we would all be mind readers.

However, what we do know for a fact is that how we talk to our self affects our outlook on life and our health. The voice of the Inner Critic is silent to the outside world, but internally its talk can be very violent and this can hold us back from achieving what we want out of life. The point I am making is that how we talk to ourselves is a learned behavior pattern. It is a habit, a habit that, thankfully, we can change.

Below are some of the anxiety-producing rules and knowledge which the Inner Critic accumulates and then stores in our unconscious mind. It then comes forward because it loves to impose itself just to de-stabilize us on an important occasion.

The Inner Critic Rules

- It knows everything about you, from your sexual thoughts to the cellulite on your thighs, and it will remind you of this just as you are about to make love.

- It remembers even the oldest and most out-of-date information such as when, aged 10, you stole a pen from a department store and it will remind you of this out-of-date data just when you are about to go for that all-important interview as the Sales Director of a department store.

- It knows every time you have felt vulnerable, such as when you have been unsuccessful at cutting down on alcohol, losing weight, going to the gym or getting that new job. And it just loves to remind you of this over and over again every time you feel the inspiration to do these things or other activities.

- It reads other people's minds for you. It's like your own personal psychic telling you what they think of you, which makes you feel insecure and less than you are.

- It will hound you day in and day out until you give in to its demands because it is frightened that if you don't listen to it, it will have failed in its job and so, of course, you listen.

- It thinks that everybody else deals with their life much better than you do, and it will constantly compare you to anybody and everybody in any situation where you feel slightly vulnerable. The Inner Critic then makes you feel extremely fearful and scared about life.

- It is the part that loves procrastination and indecisiveness and prevents you from succeeding, because it has already played out the negative scene telling you that you will fail yet again.

When you feel unsafe and feel the stir of anxiety, the Inner Critic will appear in full force for it loves vulnerability. The Inner Critic thinks and believes that if it can get in first as a protective mechanism then it is doing its work by preparing you for the worst case scenario. If you do listen to the Inner Critic, then it's guaranteed you will be hesitant with your decision making. This lack of ability to make decisions leads to self-doubt and often leaves the individual emotionally frozen, unable to pursue whatever it is they truly want to do.

Chapter 3
The Healthy Confident Part

The Stress Less Mind

The Healthy Confident Part

The good news is that there is another part of you that represents the motivated you. It is the part that bought *The Stress Less Mind* book and CD. This part is your "Healthy Confident Part." It is the part that has the resources to help move you on to create helpful, healthy responses to stress in your life. This positive part does shine through sometimes, but often, through life experiences it has been literally squashed down by the Inner Critic.

For some people the Healthy Confident Part will lay dormant for long periods of time, in particular if an ongoing stressful situation doesn't change. This is when depression may step in. The thought of being positive, confident and coping with life when you live through the eyes of the Inner Critic is virtually impossible. As the Inner Critic thinks that not liking yourself is the normal response for you it will keep the Healthy Confident Part at bay, frightened because it thinks that being positive is an unsafe experience.

The Healthy Confident Part is the part that needs to be strengthened so you can let go of anxiety and stress. You can strengthen your Healthy Confident Part through listening to *The Stress Less Mind* CD. As you do this you will begin to notice positive dialogue within you and you will discover that you will be able to respond positively and let go of stress and begin to believe in you.

The more you become aware of your Healthy Confident Part the stronger the inner energy which lies within you will become. This inner energy produces calming endorphins physically in your body. This then results in a positive domino effect as you sleep better, deal with situations better and enjoy life more!

The Goal of Your Healthy Confident Part

Over the next few chapters, you will be introduced to some new concepts; these will help you to gain an understanding of the different personality traits that we all have. In order for you to feel confident to improve your emotional life, you need to bring in your Healthy Confident Part as your strongest voice. Of all the parts within you, it is your Healthy Confident Part which will allow you to deal with life with increased energy, self-belief and self-respect, irrespective of your past. You cannot change your past but you can change your present and your future. The best way of achieving this is by listening to *The Stress Less Mind* CD. It is an integral and invaluable part of *The Stress Less Mind* book. You need to educate your Healthy Confident Part to be present in your daily life. Once it is more present, you won't feel so stressed because the lovely calming endorphins that you create will be more available to you.

Decisions

Inner Dialogue is about breaking down and understanding the inner conversations we all have with ourselves. It could be likened to you being the gardener of your own mind. The positive dialogue which you have planted through the years are the flowers, and the negative dialogue are the weeds. And so it is important for every one of us to discover, recognize and listen to the positive voice/part. As you understand and become aware of the positive and negative voices/parts you will gain important self-knowledge and begin to enjoy the positives in life. *The Stress Less Mind* will assist you to recognize the positive voice/part which supports us in our adult life, as well as discovering and recognizing the negative voice/part which is non-supportive and leads to ill health.

Discovering this process is a fun and enlightening experience, for as you begin to explore and discover your Inner Dialogue you will find yourself able to make decisions about what is right for you now. You will discover what is relevant to the way you choose to live your life, rather than living in a pattern of non-productive behavior carried forward from your past years, which prevents you from enjoying life.

Finding Wisdom and Intuition

When you have a strong Healthy Confident Part, it means that you can make healthier decisions, procrastinate less and live a happier life because you're not believing the Inner Critic to be the truth, because it is not your truth it is just a negative opinion. This knowledge in itself is powerful and rewarding because you will be managing and balancing your life with the wisdom and inner energy of your Healthy Confident Part.

It is incredible how much more intuitive you will naturally become when your Inner Critic is not your strongest voice. It is amazing how liberating experiencing this sixth sense can be as it guides you to know what is right for you and what is not. It enhances your sense of knowing which people to invite into your life and which not to.

When people are in Inner Critic mode regularly they tend to attract negative people and difficult situations into their lives. Of course, this is not necessarily a conscious decision, but when this happens the half empty glass syndrome is affirmed and life is hard and difficult as the negative cycle continues.

However, when you are living your life through the eyes, ears and the feelings of your Healthy Confident Part, it is amazing how many more opportunities you see and how many more positive situations you attract into your life. This is simply because energetically you are open to positive moments. You see beyond the limitations of your life and feel a sense of hope and trust in your present and your future. Whereas when you are in the Inner Critic mode you are closed and will rebuff positive moments because the Inner Critic will blind you with fear and anxiety.

By listening to *The Stress Less Mind* CD, you will be expanding your horizons. Therefore problems will become much easier to resolve because you are open to the positive possibilities in life. This happens because you are no longer shut down but alive with faith and trust in you. Stress then becomes less of a problem because you are managing your life with more clarity and optimism and the domino effect is that other areas of your life improve too.

The endorphins that your Healthy Confident Part produces increase and become naturally stronger while the depleting stress chemicals become less. This allows your body to feel calmer, more relaxed and you feel a sense of positive influence over your life. You will notice that you are coping better with life's anxieties or whatever difficulties come your way because you are in touch with the wisdom of your Healthy Confident Part rather than your Inner Critic.

Each moment you are in this lovely calm environment of your mind you will continually store positive new references for how to deal with life confidently without constantly living in fear, guilt and anxiety. Then this becomes the positive learned behavior through positive Inner Dialogue. This will enable you to improve the quality of your thoughts and feelings.

The New Library of Your Life

The good news is that by using *The Stress Less Mind* CD in the back of this book your mind is learning to create a new library that reflects positive thoughts and feelings. As the unconscious mind is where all of the emotional memories are stored, by listening to the CD your mind is storing positive feelings that trigger physical sensations of calm and confidence and a sense of moving out of the depths of stressful learned behaviors.

Remember, words produce feelings and feelings produce responses both positive and negative. Anger and fear produce anxiety chemicals in the body. The good news is that with the help of your Healthy Confident Part wonderful endorphins are being produced to combat any negative Radio Crazy conversations.

This may all feel beyond you at the moment, particularly if you are going through a very stressful time in your life, but these positive feelings do belong within you. Listening to *The Stress Less Mind* CD will assist your mind on how to think differently as it reacquaints itself with the positive aspects of you.

Your New Anti-Stress Pill

Your new stress management pill is *The Stress Less Mind* CD in the back of this book. Every time you listen to the CD all of these positive words are being absorbed and stored as your reference library in your unconscious mind, the deeper part of your mind. This place is where your mind and body learn to connect and relax. Think of *The Stress Less Mind* book and CD as your new anti-stress pill, one that you can take as often as you like. The more you listen to the CD, the more your mind will learn how to like yourself and let go of anxiety which leads to stress.

Positive talk can be learned and this is what you will be doing, whilst you are relaxing and chilling out while listening to *The Stress Less Mind* CD. You will be listening to positive inner conversations with me and, ultimately, once your mind gets used to this positive Inner Dialogue then you will be saying it too.

"Classic FM"

Until you educate your mind to think differently it will continue to listen to negative Radio Crazy. The dial will be stuck on this station until you direct it to another station. What you need to do is to show your mind how to tune into "Classic FM," where you are able to relax into a space of calm and peace.

In order to achieve this, repetition of listening to *The Stress Less Mind* CD is important, for as you do this you will be learning a new language of emotional wellbeing. And you will understand how to tune into your "Classic FM" inner dialogue so that it becomes a natural way of life.

Chapter 4
The Pleaser

The Stress Less Mind

What is The Pleaser?

The Pleaser is the part within us that harbors our fear of not being good enough or liked enough, this then is reflected in our sense of self-worth. If you are a Pleaser, you will notice that you spend a lot of time worrying about looking after other people to the detriment of your own health and wellbeing.

The Pleaser person is usually very stressed out because they worry too much about how other people see them as a citizen of this earth. The Pleaser part in our mind conjures up and creates a lot of stress by creating different scenarios about what people will think of us if we don't give them one hundred percent when they ask us to do something. The Pleaser part makes us feel unnecessarily guilty if we take on too much and then can't fulfill the tasks we were given and we then find ourselves in a stressful situation.

This self-induced stress is a result of not being able to say no when we need to. Not being able say no eventually depletes our necessary intuitive energy as we are too physically and emotionally exhausted to look after our self. *The Stress Less Mind* CD will help strengthen your Healthy Confident Part and enable you to connect with this positive internal energy.

Deirdre's Stress-Related Condition

Deirdre came to see me because she wasn't sleeping very well. Insomnia is a very common stress-related condition. Lack of sleep, as you may know if you have experienced it, makes the world a much more difficult place to live in. Sleep deprivation causes negative thinking and anxiety, which then becomes a Hamster Stress Wheel of low self-esteem issues as you become emotionally and physically exhausted.

Deirdre, a mother of three children had all of a sudden become an insomniac. She couldn't put her finger on just why this had happened, all she knew was that one night she couldn't sleep. A year had gone by since that first sleepless night and it was driving her crazy, and her husband too.

I explained to Deirdre if sleep is an issue then there will usually be an underlying anxiety that triggers the insomnia. The interesting irony of this condition is that the mind assumes that staying awake will resolve the problem and yet it makes the problem worse because in the morning you get out of bed exhausted. Unless we have a clear and rested mind, problem solving is difficult. In fact, it creates more problems because we have been on the Hamster Stress Wheel all night and we are too exhausted both emotionally and physically to look at the problem clearly.

I asked Deirdre to recall the time the insomnia started and was there anything that may have created the thought that staying awake was a good thing for her to do. She was stuck for a while until I gave her a few examples of other clients with insomniac problems. Then she had a light bulb moment and this is what she said: "I feel embarrassed to say this but I think it may have to do with my daughter going to a new school. We decided that our eldest daughter who is very academically bright should go to a private girls' school."

Deirdre continued saying that her daughter was having problems settling in at the private school and she felt guilty that she and her husband had taken her out of a school where she had been happy. She also said she was embarrassed and upset because she felt that they were the poor family of the school. Most of the girls' parents appeared much wealthier than they were and her daughter had suggested this too.

In order for Deirdre to feel liked by the mothers she had gone out of her way to make friends with them while at the same time she was running herself ragged because she said yes to every social event as well as taking on other parents' responsibilities. She did all of this so that she would be accepted. At this stage Deirdre broke down crying. She told me she felt a failure to her daughter as well her new-found friends because she felt she was never good enough or could not do enough for the mothers at her daughter's new school. Deirdre continued, "I lie awake at night worried about whether I said and did the right thing. And then when I pick my daughter up from school I begin to worry about dropping her off in the morning. I feel I have to work so much harder to fit in and be liked and it is exhausting. My husband doesn't help because he just says, 'stop worrying and go to sleep.' It's easy for him to say that!"

Deirdre was a classic Pleaser, so it was little wonder that she was not sleeping. Her Pleaser kept telling her she had to keep everyone happy in order for her and her daughter to be accepted by both the parents and her daughter's peer group. And so Deirdre said yes to everything these people asked of her whether it was convenient or not. As a result she exhausted herself pleasing others because she believed this was the way to be accepted and liked.

The Word "NO"

Pleasers have a real problem saying no and Deirdre had all the classic signs of this behavior. All of the efforts borne out of her desire to make sure her and her daughter were accepted made her try to achieve everything, and along the way she forgot about herself, which is a common problem of the Pleaser personality.

I respected that Deirdre justifiably as a mother had concerns about her daughter's welfare and this was perfectly normal. However, underpinning this anxiety was the fear that not only might she be rejected by the other school mothers she also believed that her daughter would never forgive her for moving her and placing her in a new school.

Deirdre's Pleaser kept coming up with and creating all these different crazy scenarios of rejection which filled her with anxiety and fear. She believed that she had to do what the mothers at the school were doing, and that included spending money that she and her husband didn't have.

The word "no" stirs too many fearful thoughts in the Pleaser as they fear they will be rejected, abandoned and left out. So they go out of their way to make sure they are one hundred percent useful and available for every function and social duty that comes their way.

Deirdre's desperation for her and her daughter to belong had become detrimental to her own health and wellbeing. These health issues are a common Pleaser problem, and for Deirdre it began by manifesting itself so that it kept her awake at night so that she developed insomnia.

Feeling Used

I asked Deirdre had she ever felt used in her life. She looked a little uncomfortable with the question and then she scanned her mind and said, "I wouldn't say 'used' but there have been times where I have felt that people have taken advantage of my good nature." This is a very predictable Pleaser response. Pleasers do not like to admit that they have been used because they see it as a sign of weakness.

Pleasers are notorious for living in fear that they will be criticized because they need to be liked. So they say yes to everything and in the process take on too much and Deirdre was no exception.

The Irony of the Pleaser

Most people love having a Pleaser person in their lives because they do the things the other person doesn't like doing. Pleasers say yes to everything because they are frightened that if they say no, they will be rejected. The irony of this is that, deep down, the fear of being rejected is actually more important to the Pleaser than the person they are pleasing, and this is the reason they say yes. If they say no to the other person then their Pleaser will say, internally, "That person is offended" or "If you don't say yes, they may not ask you again and then you won't have any friends."

The Pleaser part of your personality revels in making you feel bad if you take time out for yourself. For the Pleaser does not allow you to value yourself.

Pleasers are constantly checking in with people to make sure they are okay, rather than checking in with themselves, because they don't see themselves as important enough. They constantly undervalue themselves and overvalue the people around them.

Deirdre needed to bring in the energy of her Healthy Confident Part to support her to sleep. I made her a personalized recording, which I do for all my private clients. I call this unconscious homework. I asked her to listen to the CD when she was ready to go to sleep as it was her Pleaser that was keeping her awake with all of its guilt-ridden stories, so it was important to combat this anxiety by calming her while building her Healthy Confident Part. I explained to Deirdre that hypnosis is the natural stage we all go through before we go to sleep at night and that the CD was the perfect bedtime story for her to listen to.

The CD was also training Deirdre's mind to do something for herself. As Pleasers are not very good at looking after themselves this was a great way to encourage Deirdre to take strong, small steps towards sleeping as well as learning to value herself.

I also gave Deirdre some conscious homework where she had to say no to just one person. She was horrified that she would have to do this, but I said the only way she was going to improve her emotional life was to start by having a little bit of courage to change. I gave her a few examples of how she could practice her assertiveness beginning with calmly, positively and politely saying no to certain people such as the bossy customer in the local shop who made her feel uncomfortable when he pushed his way before her in the queue. All she needed to do was to say to him, "Excuse me, I was here first."

Deirdre came bouncing in the next week having had a great week of sleep. She said that she was very impressed with herself because one of the mothers at the school who asked a lot from Deirdre wanted her to pick up her daughter and drop her off with her ex-husband because she didn't want to see his new girlfriend and Deirdre had said calmly and politely, "No." I was so proud of her, but more importantly she was proud of herself.

The Charming Pleaser

The purpose of the Pleaser is to keep everybody else happy. It is the part that makes sure everyone else's needs are met first. The Pleaser's personality is often charming, open and warm to the outside world. It is a very attractive character trait to have because you will be well liked. The down side is the more you look after someone else, the less time you have to look after you.

Pleasers are endearing to many people because of their charm; however, being charming on the outside is different to what is going on on the inside, which is often an angry, seething person because they do not have their needs met. This is one of the major problems of the Pleaser, as they do not voice themselves by saying no they stew over everything and everyone who they say yes to.

Pleasers are Popular People

Pleasers are lovely people because they are good listeners and will always entertain the idea of coordinating other people's lives because they need to be useful. The shame of it is that by keeping busy pleasing others, the Pleaser has no time left energetically or emotionally for pleasing themselves.

Deirdre recognized that pleasing too much was causing her insomnia and that she was the only person who could resolve her sleeping problem. Being popular because you are a Pleaser can be lovely, but it is also places a burden on you because people become used to relying on you too much.

Pleasers and Money in Abundance

Pleasers are always spending money on other people because it is a way of being liked and respected. Unfortunately, they do this because they don't respect themselves and then they find themselves in some serious pickles, and one of these is being short of money. They pay for other people's meals and buy drinks for scrooge-type people who are mean with money in the false belief that this will make the other person feel better as well as making the Pleaser feel better.

The flip side to this is that scrooge people love having Pleasers in their lives because their bill always gets paid, of course, by the Pleaser.

How Other People View You

If you have a strong Pleaser trait then you will have low self-esteem and this will be reflected in overdoing things for other people. This is done unconsciously because it helps you avoid looking at yourself. You actually don't want to take the time to look at what is driving you to please other people. Often the Pleaser is a person who sees themselves as useless.

Your self-esteem relies on how other people view you and not on how you view yourself. This is one of the major problems of the Pleaser. The Pleaser part is constantly badgering you to make sure you are liked so that you will be accepted and yet the most important thing is for you to accept and like yourself, then you will be liked and valued by others.

Pleasers Can Be Martyrs

Pleasers can become very irritating to other people because they can become martyrs without consciously realizing it. When other people offer to help the Pleaser they will constantly be rebuffed because the Pleaser likes to think they can do it all and the truth is they can't. The result is that people stop offering their help because they become tired of the Pleaser's martyrdom. Everyone needs help at some point in their life. Pleasers are not forthcoming at relinquishing what they perceive as their responsibility because secretly they think that if they don't have things to do then they will become redundant. Pleasers will often mistakenly martyr themselves because they believe this will impress other people.

Making Decisions

Making important decisions for the Pleaser can be a problem as they will not trust their own sense of what is right, rather they will take on the opinions of people around them. They will back away from using their intuitive sense of what is right to please others and often this leads to further feelings of inadequacy. Making decisions for the Pleaser becomes a stressful chore because they need continuous confirmation that they are not seen as silly or foolish. Pleasers need a lot of reassurance that their decision was the right one and will often back away from making a decision which they know will be beneficial but unpopular, so that they continue to be liked.

Food and Alcohol

Pleasers like to over-indulge in food and alcohol. At the end of a busy day they will be exhausted and often the only way to have their needs met is to overeat and drink too much. This is their way to escape the pressures of life. Pleasers are so busy rushing around looking after everybody else that sometimes food and alcohol are the only way they can relax and shut off from the outside world.

Pleasers may also use food and alcohol as a way to numb down their anger as their voice is not being heard. They literally may stuff down too much food or drink in an all out effort to push their angry feelings away. As Pleasers feel guilty about most things, escaping their lives by over-indulging can become their stress management tool, for this is their coping strategy.

This coping strategy is extremely common and if it continues to be the Pleaser's stress management pill then serious health issues can occur as this can lead to weight gain and alcohol dependency. When this happens then those people who are around can be at a loss as to how to help the over-indulging Pleaser.

Pleasers are also very good at making sure a small amount of food can stretch to feeding 10. They are like the good Girl Guide or Boy Scout for they always make sure that everyone is fed and watered. They have great peripheral vision for multi-tasking at all times and this means that they don't miss anything.

Pleasers are great at parties both as hosts and guests because they will make sure everyone has enough to eat and drink and will be on full-time alert to anyone standing in the corner looking shy. They are great at the art of conversation and that is why people love having Pleasers at their party because they will keep the conversation flowing. Pleasers loath silences, they will see it as a reflection of them, rather than the fact that perhaps people just don't have anything to say, so they will fill the gaps of conversation where possible.

The Pleaser and Sex

Pleasers are often seen as being promiscuous because they can have a lot sexual partners. They desperately want to be accepted and loved so they often make the mistake that when someone asks them for sex they will say yes, not because they want to have sex but rather they don't want to offend. Pleasers can be confused about sex because on one hand they think that by saying yes the other person won't feel rejected. On the other hand they love being loved so can often mistake sex for love. Then when they are rejected after a one night stand they feel confused, hurt and unloved, and this makes them feel let down and their self-esteem plummets and then they begin to question what more they could have done to make that person love them.

Mary's Story

Mary's father was a judgmental man who constantly criticized her mother. Mary lived in fear of her father criticizing her too because she could see how upset her mother would get. To protect her mother Mary would make her feel better by trying to do things for her so her father wouldn't pick on her. Unfortunately Mary's protection didn't always work, in particular when she was told to go to bed by her father and stop meddling in their business.

Mary continued to behave like this in all aspects of her life and at the age of 42 she came to see me and what I saw was a nervous wreck.

Mary was a classic Pleaser who lived on the edge of her seat, living in fear of being criticized at any time. I very rarely say this but Mary was one of the worst Pleasers I had ever met. She had avoided so many aspects of her life that would have enhanced her life. She had plenty of friends, or should I say people who she ran around after, but her life was very empty.

Mary had never had a committed relationship. She said she did try but never felt comfortable with men as she always connected men with being unkind and lacking in patience.

Mary's unconscious mind had created a habit of feeling unsafe around men. Mary cleverly trained to be a teacher in a girls' school so she very rarely had to deal with male authority. So in Mary's eyes she was safe.

The reason why Mary came to see me was because she was sick and tired of herself not taking any risks in life and she, in fact, had feelings for one of the male teachers at the school that were stirring lots of good feelings which was making her feel stressed.

Mary's fear was incredibly high and yet you could see the excitement in her eyes as she talked about this man at work who she clearly had a crush on. It was going to be a definite strong, small step process for Mary to start living the life she truly wanted, but she had put her hand up to do something by coming to see me and that was the first big step.

As mentioned in the introduction chapter, one of the great tools hypnosis can give you straight away is to feel the energy of the Healthy Confident Part simply by listening to the CD in the back of the book. You will start to notice how much safer you feel and how much less stressed or bothered by anxiety you are because your body cannot produce both stress and calm chemicals at the same time. It has to make a choice.

Mary's mind was learning with the aid of the hypnosis to disconnect from those old, out-of-date feelings that men were all critical and judgmental. She was also learning to equate emotionally that when around the energy of men, in particular single and available men, she started to feel a sense of excitement. I gave her homework that she needed to do on the train morning and night of noticing men and looking at them while connecting to safe feelings.

Mary came to see me a few weeks later and said she was feeling better in herself; however, the loveliest thing was that she was starting to feel sexually turned on by men. She said she had never experienced this before because it was always unsafe.

Be Careful of Who Your Real Friends Are

As Pleasers are very good at making sure everybody else is okay, they will have a lot of friends who expect a lot from them. Pleasers, as I mentioned, are popular. However, they often have friends who are bullish and demand a lot from them. Often when the Pleaser is in need of help, for instance if they are ill, then they find out who their real friends are. Selfish or bullish friends are soon found out and the reason for this is that the Pleaser is no longer available for their use and so they don't bother with the Pleaser. These people are not very good at reciprocating unconditional kindness.

The Pleaser can easily become disillusioned about life when they are let down in certain circumstances by people they perceived were friends. These feelings of disillusionment also occur in the work environment when they feel let down by certain colleagues they have been helpful to. They just can't understand how other people can be cruel and inconsiderate when they have been kind and generous.

When the Chips Are Down

When the chips are down it is interesting to find out who really likes and values you for being you rather than for what you can offer them. Matt, a client of mine questioned this not so long ago when he came to see me with depression. Matt had made a lot of money as a property developer at a very young age and had mixed in the upper rich circle of society. A once very popular person, after making a few bad business decisions he lost everything along with his so-called friends.

Matt's once flash lifestyle now was nowhere to be found. He had moved in with his sister to try and sort out what he was going to do with his life and it was his sister who suggested that he came to see me.

Matt was completely stressed out and at a loss as to how people could just drop him as a friend. As he said to me, "I would never do that. First thing I would do is help my friend get back on their feet, not dump them." Matt went on to say that there was one friend who he had loaned money to that now refused to return his calls while still living the high life that he had helped this so-called friend to build.

Disappearing Friends

People and their reactions, in particular with money situations, are quite fascinating. I have noticed that when a client's financial or professional life changes for the worst, it is almost like they have a disease and some of their so-called friends disappear and go underground. It is terrible to see how some people treat others due to position and money. When the person is up there living the high life then they are part of the elite group; however, if one of these people falls on hard times then they are often shut out from the world they knew. Instead of being embraced and helped they are rejected and this is what happened to Matt.

Matt felt so alone and completely abandoned and I could see how important it was to rebuild his self-esteem. To accomplish this we needed to work with his Healthy Confident Part so that he could see that the situation he now found himself in was temporary. To accomplish this Matt needed to develop his intuitive self so that he would make wiser choices in his friendships.

The stressful situation Matt now found himself in was compounded by his Pleaser being joined by his Inner Critic. The combination of these two parts created within Matt serious and dangerous stress levels. His Inner Critic kept telling him he was a loser and his Pleaser kept asking him why his friends had rejected him. No wonder Matt was stressed, his Radio Crazy had placed him in internal conflict and had seriously got the better of him.

Pleasing Yourself

When a person begins to work with their Pleaser it can have an interesting effect which could be likened to throwing a pebble into a lake; through this action circles radiate out and relationship dynamics can change. A bully for example will be drawn to a Pleaser-type personality because they know they can get away with bad behavior. A Pleaser will be attracted to a bully because they are always trying to get their approval and please them, which very rarely happens. It is no wonder that when a Pleaser starts to gain confidence that the bully in the relationship is not happy.

Michelle came to see me about losing weight. She was married and had not been able to conceive a child and this had become a big problem in their relationship. They had tried IVF a few times without success and as a result of this Michelle's husband had decided that if they couldn't have their own children then they would not have any children. Michelle had different thoughts, but every time she mentioned adoption to her husband he would dismiss her saying that the discussion was closed.

I asked Michelle how she felt about this and she simply shrugged her shoulders and said, "I married him and if he doesn't want to adopt what can I do?" I asked if her weight had anything to do with not being able to become a mother and she said yes and that she and her husband had become very distant and she now only had sex as a dutiful chore. It was clear that Michelle felt trapped and was emotionally overeating to compensate for the loss of potential children.

Michelle's stress levels were of concern because they were high and depression had set in. I asked her if she knew how unhappy she appeared to be and she admitted that she was at a loss as to how to find herself again amongst the excess weight that she had put on.

I talked to Michelle about her Pleaser personality and her reply was that she had spent all her life looking after everybody else and that she could never imagine this changing. It was important for Michelle to see that her husband had bullied her into the decision of not adopting and that they needed to discuss this together and that while her voice was not being heard within their relationship she would never be happy and nor would the relationship. I certainly wasn't suggesting that Michelle should demand to adopt a child but rather take strong, small steps towards being more assertive with him. Once she did this then she would feel more equal in their relationship and this would then lead to her feeling more free.

I really wanted Michelle to see that by holding back from voicing herself she was creating her own inner stress and it certainly wasn't helpful to her or her husband. From what Michelle said, her husband appeared not to be interested in anything that Michelle had to say or wanted to do and this was not only about potential children. Through not voicing herself Michelle had let her husband assume that what he wanted was all-important.

It was crunch time for Michelle and she knew it. I suggested that she listen to her personalized CD as much as she could as this would help support her goal of becoming more confident in voicing what she wanted and needed.

Pleasers Can Be Aggressive

Michelle, like many Pleasers, harbored festering anger. Once the Pleaser anger builds up it erupts in a volcanic crescendo and spews forth anger like molten lava, so you better run a mile from this aggressive anger. It takes a lot for a Pleaser to blow their fuse but when they do you better take cover!

Michelle was worried that once she started explaining to her husband about how she felt that all the anger and resentment she had hidden deep inside would come out and she would be too aggressive. In the past Michelle had always drunk alcohol to find the courage to express herself, so I encouraged her to trust that she wouldn't need alcohol once her Healthy Confident Part was more present in her life. We rehearsed in hypnosis the feeling of calm to help produce the healthy endorphins while having Michelle say something upbeat while being assertive. Rehearsing this way prepared Michelle to enable her to stay calm at the same time as being positively assertive as she talked with her husband.

Alcohol and Assertiveness

Pleasers, when socializing, often need to over-drink because this means they can say things to people which they wouldn't say when sober. Pleasers, due to their lack of assertiveness, will drink to express their real opinion. I believe this is another common reason why people over-consume alcohol. People drink to release their suppressed inner fears and when the lid is off they let fly and behave in a way that they would not normally do.

The Pleaser represents within us a deep-rooted fear of not being liked. If you use alcohol to free these fears then you can often find yourself in deep water. There is a very real danger for the Pleaser who uses alcohol to free their tongue to express their opinions, for they run the risk of becoming caught in a vicious cycle of drinking which then becomes a problem.

Unfortunately, for the Pleaser this alcohol-fuelled freedom of angry, explosive speech rarely seems to be with the person they need to confront, instead it is often a bewildered, innocent bystander who cops the explosion. On the other hand, alcohol can give them the false confidence to confront the person which they would not have the courage to do sober. And so they can become aggressively unreasonable which does more harm than good and accomplishes little except regret in the morning when the Inner Critic kicks in to berate them for what they said and did the night before.

Michelle returned to see me a few weeks later and it was clear to me that she had lost weight. She was really thrilled with her progress not just with her weight but with the fact that she had been able to sit down with her husband and explain to him that she wasn't happy and that they both needed to make more of an effort in the relationship. Her husband wasn't so sure about his newly confident wife, but I told her that in time he would hopefully get used to the new Michelle.

Not Everybody Supports Positive Change

The following week Michelle came in not so happy. I asked her what was wrong and she replied that her husband who had always been critical of her excess weight and always commented when she ate fattening food, came home one night with her favorite meal, a meal he had never allowed her to eat. It was burger and fries. I looked at her and we both knew then that he was feeling very uncomfortable and threatened by his new slim, confident wife and so he had set about trying to sabotage Michelle through her love of food.

It is extremely common when a Pleaser finds their Healthy Confident Part that the relationship dynamics they have with others undergo a significant change. Some people cope and enjoy being with this new person and the relationship grows whether it is a friend or partner, while other people respond negatively because it rocks their boat and they feel threatened. It is most important that the Pleaser understands that being stressed and unhappy is not an okay way to live especially if the person who is causing the stress is getting away with sabotaging, controlling and manipulative bad behavior.

It is important that the Pleaser evaluates what it is that keeps them in a relationship that is not healthy and therefore stressful for them. Michelle faced the fact that her husband wanted to be the ultimate decision maker in the relationship. He didn't want a sharing relationship, he wanted control. He didn't want to adopt children and would not discuss it. He criticized her for being overweight and eating fatty food, but when she lost weight and gained confidence he tried to undermine her by offering her the very food he criticized her for eating. As Michelle grew in confidence and her stress levels began to drop away she faced the fact that if her husband was continually criticizing and putting her down that he was in fact a verbal bully. Eventually after months of trying to cope with the stressful situation Michelle made the painful but healthy choice to leave. She gave herself time out to really look at what it was that she wanted out of life. This was a brave move for Michelle; however, with a little bit of courage Michelle's life dramatically improved and attracted a healthy relationship into her life.

White Lies

Lies are not something I encourage; however, for Pleasers a little white lie may occasionally become a necessity. When a Pleaser wants to practice being assertive telling a white lie is a good stepping stone towards self-expression in a positive way. A person might try to sabotage the Pleaser's new-found confidence by trying to goad them into eating a cream cake when they are trying to stay off fattening food. This is the time when the Pleaser could say, "Oh, I just had a big piece of cake before I left the office and I can't fit another piece in. I'll just have coffee."

Pleasers love voice mail, emails and texting and although it may seem a little gutless it is a great way to learn to say no to people because you are not dealing with them face to face. Other people think nothing of using these devices to say no and the Pleaser can benefit from using this non-confronting form of conversation when learning to say no.

If someone asks you to do something that you genuinely know you can't or don't want to do then take a step back and decide not to decide at that moment. All you need to do to accomplish this is simply say, "I'll have to get back to you" and then leave it for a time before deciding if you really want to do what they are asking you to do. Take some time out to practice saying no. Write down why you cannot or do not want to do what they want you to do at that particular point in time. The reason for writing these answers down is that it will become clear to you why you can't or don't want to do it and more than likely you will find you have a valid reason. This will strengthen your resolve that it is okay to say no. Doing this may seem difficult at first, but it will give you clarity as to why you have the right to say no. Then all you need to do is make the excuse politely as to why you cannot do what they want.

It does take practice, but as I have said everything always does. The more you practice in your mind being assertive then the more your mind knows that it is safe to do this.

Pleasers' Own Problems

Pleasers are not keen on honestly expressing how they feel about their lives to other people. The Pleaser part finds this uncomfortable. The reason for this is because the Pleaser part thinks if other people know their vulnerability then they may not like them or that they will not be there to help them. Pleasers are always saying they are fine, and yet most of the time they are not. They are so busy swimming in their own low self-esteem that they do not value themselves as much as other people do. This low self-worth then leads to moodiness and a sense of wanting to hibernate from the outside world. Pleasers need to retreat from time to time, simply to re-charge their batteries, and sleep is a way of achieving this.

Another way for the Pleaser to escape pleasing other people is being ill. Many Pleasers get ill due to exhaustion and when they get ill they can get extremely ill. This happens because they are so busy running around pleasing that they do not have the time to read the signs that their body is giving them. Then there are some Pleasers who see illness as the only legitimate way to get genuine help and attention from other people without asking for it.

Inability to Ask for Help

If you are a Pleaser, asking for help is generally a big issue. You are great at saying yes to everyone else, but opening up to your own problems and sharing them with others is unacceptable. This is because the Pleaser is worried that if people know their fears and vulnerabilities then they won't want to hang around them. They fear that these people will not be understanding enough or strong enough to help them with their own problems.

Friends and family get tired of asking if a Pleaser is alright because they always get the same answer: "I'm fine" even when they are not. So is it any wonder that after a while people stop asking a Pleaser how they are?

Pete's father died when he was 16 and he learned very quickly to become the man of the house. In order to protect his mother he became the "strong" one of the family and unconsciously decided that always being reliable, kind, honest and hardworking was essential to keep his mother safe. Being kind, honest and reliable are wonderful qualities in a human being and are the mainstay of healthy relationships; however, Pete took it to the maximum.

By the time Pete walked through my clinic door he was extremely tearful. His girlfriend had insisted that he make an appointment to see me because he was being bullied at university by an older student.

Pleasers, as I mentioned, do not like admitting they have problems and will often make jokes to hide their vulnerabilities – Pete was no exception. He insisted that he was fine and that the only reason he came to see me was to please his girlfriend!

Pete and I spent the first appointment training his mind to have more self-confidence so that he was able to report this bully to the university. He agreed he would do this and fortunately he did. As it turned out this bully had been harassing many other students and once warned didn't do it again.

The great aspect of Pete recognizing his Pleaser wasn't helping him meant he gained more confidence to express himself and say no when he wanted to without fear, anxiety and guilt. He even learned to stand his ground with his girlfriend who found this added to their relationship as Pete no longer tried to ingratiate himself all the time with her. Their conversations became more enlightened as they explored and expressed their own opinions.

The Assertive Positive Pleaser

The Pleaser part has so much to offer as it has a genuine desire to be kind, warm, fair and love unconditionally. If you look at all the qualities the Pleaser has to offer then you can see for yourself what a wonderful asset it can be for you and for others. Pleasers, just imagine what would happen if you started to nurture yourself instead of continually nurturing other people. Think of how your life would be less stressed if you learned to say no. You probably may experience a little bit of uneasiness stirring inside you when I suggest you nurture yourself and this is because the Pleaser is concerned that if you look after yourself then you will be rejected by other people. It is completely normal for a Pleaser to feel this way and I would be surprised if you didn't feel these uncomfortable stirrings regarding nurturing yourself so you can discover your Healthy Confident Self. If you do not have feelings of uneasiness with the suggestion of nurturing yourself then congratulations for you do not have a strong Pleaser!

Training Your Pleaser to Spend Time Out

At first, looking after you can be a little bit stressful and a little testing as people adjust to you taking time for you. However, the people you know will get used to it and you will, too. If someone doesn't like you saying no or taking time out then the relationship clearly is not a supportive one and you may need to change it anyway. This process is like starting a new relationship; however, this time it is with yourself.

The Pleaser Can Work With You

What a pleasure it is to still look after people with the knowledge that the caring comes from your own choice rather than from fear. The good news is that having a Pleaser personality means that you will always be interested in other people and the world around you. Pleasers love exploring new ideas because it aids them in their conversation and giving advice. Pleasers are much loved and their contribution to the world is limitless when they understand how to arrive confidently at their inner place of strength and energetically and intuitively follow their beliefs to help others.

Listening to *The Stress Less Mind* CD accompanying this book will help you contact and connect with your energetic and intuitive Healthy Confident Self, which will enable you to give to others without depleting your own life-giving vital energy.

Chapter 5
The Perfectionist

The Stress Less Mind

The Perfectionist

What is the Perfectionist?

The Perfectionist is the part of you that has one very strict rule which you must abide by. And its rule is that you must achieve one hundred percent, and if you can't achieve one hundred percent then the Perfectionist tells you that you are a failure.

Often people say to me, "I am not a Perfectionist" and yet there will be an area of their life that is totally driven by their Perfectionist part. This could be achieving a high pass in an exam or perhaps running and finishing a marathon. There is a lot of power and determination behind the Perfectionist, which is a good thing because it makes sure we apply ourselves diligently to what we undertake; however, there is also a down side to the Perfectionist which can be detrimental to our self-worth and confidence, and cause us undue stress.

Often a strong Perfectionist part will override the weaker Pleaser part or, alternatively, if you have a strong Pleaser part, then the Perfectionist part will not be as powerful. However, it has been my experience that both these parts make their presence felt in different aspects of our life, as well as in different moments in our life.

Easy to Say No

Both the Perfectionist and the Pleaser can keep themselves extremely busy; however, there is a very big difference in how they do this.

Perfectionists are much more selfish in how they spend their time. They are very good at saying no and feel guilt free in doing this. They are good at analyzing when to say yes because they always weigh up "what's in it for them" and if there isn't something in it for them there is a high chance they will say no.

Decision Making is Easy

Perfectionists are great at making decisions because they are always sure before they make progress in their lives. They will study situations before they step into them until they are completely sure that it will be one hundred percent successful. If you are a Perfectionist then this will usually stand you in good stead because you will do your research beforehand so you always have the right information and therefore there will be minimal risk attached.

The Perfectionist Creation

The Perfectionist, like all the different parts within us, was created from early childhood to protect us and keep us safe from any perceived mishaps. When we acknowledge how these different parts operate within our unconscious mind we free ourselves to move forward positively, this then enables us to recognize any unnecessary stress these parts have created so we can restore inner harmony.

Listening to *The Stress Less Mind* CD regularly will help you recognize when you are placing yourself in stressful situations and how to resolve this stress through being aware of what is going on around you and within you. The following story of Joe will further help you become aware of whether you have a strong or mild Perfectionist part.

Joe grew up in a whirlwind of parental inconsistency. Joe knew his parents loved him but he felt let down by them because they never stuck at anything. His father and mother were both creative people and often the house was a mess. They slept late, they ate late and everything always seemed too unpredictable for Joe.

This parental inconsistency triggered within Joe a lot of anxiety and fear because he never felt safe. His mother was always trying new things and once flew to India to attend a yoga retreat and suddenly, after years of eating meat, his mother started preparing vegetarian food for the family to eat.

Joe decided at a very young age that he wanted to be different to his parents. He wanted a life where he wasn't jumping all over the place starting this and not finishing that. He wanted to know what it felt like to have predictability in his life and so he set about mapping his life out.

Joe, in his adult world, was very methodical and did not like surprises, for it triggered too much emotional stress from his past. However, as we know, life can be unpredictable and this was causing a lot of stress in his romantic life.

At university Joe met and fell in love with Kate. He loved Kate because she knew exactly what she wanted and was meticulous in her apartment and her life.

Their relationship was fiery to say the least. There was a lot of passion as well as anxiety and stress. Both were Perfectionists, which meant both found it difficult to back down when they thought they were right, and this caused a great deal of communication problems.

Joe and Kate regularly broke up and then got back together again. The make-ups were wild and passionate until they broke up the next time. It was a rollercoaster of a relationship full of inconsistency and this was ironic considering that Joe liked and wanted consistency.

Joe and Kate struggled on and off for years and then Joe started an affair with one of the girls in the office and it was this that prompted him to see me. I asked him what it was that attracted him to this girl and he replied that he liked her because she was so laid back and very relaxed about life.

I explained to Joe that in order for him to feel happy within himself he needed to realize that there is no perfect person and this included himself. It was important for Joe to understand that he was going from one relationship that he had deemed perfect and then not perfect. And now having an affair seemed right too. He was polarized in his thinking as he went from one end of the spectrum to the other. For Joe there were no half measures. It was all or nothing.

Joe needed to find some balance in his perspective and to learn how to be more accepting of other people. He was far from perfect and Joe knew this and yet he expected everybody else to be perfect. I challenged Joe about his perspective because it appeared to me he really did love Kate. He just needed to learn how to be more relaxed, more trusting and to accept the different qualities in people.

Through hypnosis we concentrated on releasing Joe's fear of being let down and how to feel safer so he could learn to take life as it comes. For it was the unpredictably of life that worried him and because of this he was frightened to let things go, which created tremendous stress. Through his stress Joe himself created stressful situations. It was a double-edged sword. What Joe needed to do was to take life in his stride and be more adaptable so he could enjoy the flow of life. He needed to bring his Healthy Confident Part to the fore so he could be more present and learn how to trust himself so he could let go of fear and relax more about life.

I am always amazed at how powerful the mind is and how it wants to protect, in its own way, the very person it also has the propensity to destroy. Unconsciously our mind can be detrimental to the life we lead. It is no surprise how people create their own stress and anxieties throughout their lives. This happens because they are not aware of how their unconscious mind chatters, which affects whether they reach their full potential. *The Stress Less Mind* has been written so you can open your eyes to how and why the stress you create can hold you back from feeling great about you. This stress prevents you from connecting with your Healthy Confident Part for it is this part that guides you intuitively to assess and connect with the situations and people you want in your life.

Setting Goals

We all have a Perfectionist trait to some extent, whether it is to make sure we look our best for the Christmas party or making sure we have done our homework on the company who are just about to interview us. Having a Perfectionist drive is healthy. The problems occur when some of the goals the Perfectionist sets are unrealistic and even if we do achieve these goals, when we get there we find sometimes they are not sustainable.

Joe realized that he did love Kate and decided to end the affair before it harmed all three of them. His Healthy Confident Part increased and he became less of a Perfectionist and began to enjoy, little by little, the unforeseen challenges that life threw his way.

Ben's Story

Ben attended one of my Stress Less Mind workshops. Throughout the morning he looked like he didn't want to be part of the group; however, as soon as I started talking about the Perfectionist he began to get fidgety. Ben knew he was stressed but he didn't know why until I mentioned the Perfectionist personality trait.

This was a loud bell ringing moment for Ben and then he said to the group, "I am definitely not a Pleaser, although I am aware I have an Inner Critic but that has never worried me because I don't feel it is that strong. I wasn't really sure whether I was attending the right stress course but now I understand it is my Perfectionist that causes my stress levels to rise." Ben went on to say that he was highly driven and was extremely frustrated because he had always been told that although he was a good worker he was not a team player.

Ben had gone from one company to the next because he felt they never did anything the right way and that he could always do it better. Then the light bulb moment struck and Ben realized that his expectations were too high for everybody in his life to do everything exactly the way he wanted them to.

Inflexibility of Perfectionists

As Perfectionists are inflexible and are not easily adaptable, they will usually have to attract people into their lives who support this behavior. Usually it is a Pleaser because they say yes rather than say no and, of course, will agree to keep the peace.

If you strive to achieve and have great success and expect those around you to be the same, then I guarantee you will not be the most popular person, but you will have a lot of people who respect your sense of drive.

Perfectionists do have friends, particularly those who agree with them or are as highly driven as they are, because they understand each other. It is like an unspoken mutual respect society. It also, on an unconscious level, keeps the Perfectionist safe to seek out other Perfectionists because they know how predictable other Perfectionists can be.

Perfectionists Can Be Well Respected

You will notice if you are driven to succeed one hundred percent that people will find your tenacity very attractive. People are drawn to you because they know when you say something you do really mean it and therefore they know where they stand. It could be likened to travelling with an experienced sea captain who has the chartered maps prepared in case of stormy weather.

Perfectionists Are Lousy Losers

Perfectionists set themselves amazing goals that they want to achieve. And they are very good at achieving them, but when things don't go to plan all hell can break loose. As they have no patience they will have little time for those who don't get what it is that they want to achieve. Their "blood boils" when they don't achieve the outcome they want. They are poor losers for they don't understand why they didn't achieve the top mark in an exam or win that tennis match. If they don't win then you'd better hide because they'll vent their rage because they feel they have failed to be perfect.

Perfectionists are great to work with because they get the job done; however, their idea of what perfect is can be very different to yours. If you are a Perfectionist you often can get very mad at other people because they don't see the minor details that you do.

It is incredibly stressful for the Perfectionist to have to deal with sloppy people and when they set goals they generally either have a team on board who are in tip top emotional condition to weather the Perfectionist expectations, or they get kicked out.

The Perfectionist does not have patience or tolerance of people who say they can do something then don't live up to their high expectations. They can be incredibly insensitive to those who are not high achievers or do not have the same emotional philosophy of life such as, "Just get it right the first time and you will be okay."

All or Nothing

The Perfectionist has a real issue with the gray area of life. They think of everything as either black or white and there is no in between. The Perfectionist relationship within a person can often drive that person to extreme lengths to achieve their goals. This applies particularly to the Perfectionist who sets a goal to lose weight. They will decide what diet they are going to follow then stick to it religiously. They will count each calorie or gram of fat and will not waiver in their determination to lose weight. When they reach their goal they often go back to eating the way they used to. These Perfectionist dieters don't understand why they are so good at losing weight and yet are so good at putting it all back on again. My book *The Weight Less Mind* explains in great detail the complexities of weight gain and loss. However, just for this Perfectionist chapter, rest assured if you are a yo-yo dieter then you will have a strong Perfectionist behind this often seemingly erratic behavior.

Many of my clients who are driven by the Perfectionist can become very frustrated with themselves because they do not understand this all or nothing syndrome.

The Inner Critic and Its Relationship with Success

If the Perfectionist part in you expects you to perform at a one hundred percent success rate at whatever goal you have set yourself, then it will scan your unconscious mind to prove you can achieve it. The Perfectionist does not allow you to do things by halves.

One of the unconscious mind's purposes is to protect you against vulnerability. If you do not have the evidence of this protection then your unconscious mind will not allow you to go there because your Perfectionist fears failure. And what happens when you fail? You feel scared, anxious, stressed out and low self-esteem sets in. Is it any surprise that sometimes it seems beyond your understanding as to why you can't achieve something, particularly if it seems easy for other people to achieve?

The good news is that *The Stress Less Mind* will help you re-train your mind so that you can achieve balance to enable you to work and live with people who may fall short of your perfection, so you will become less stressed. Remember, there is not one perfect person on this earth, including you.

Your mind has experienced great highs and lows and now it is learning through reading this book and listening to *The Stress Less Mind* CD that change is good and that achieving whatever you want is possible; however, this time it will be with wisdom rather than stress, anxiety and fear.

Perfectionist Traits Lead to Excessiveness

The Perfectionist trait can be exhausting because it has so many rules and regulations that often lead to questioning behavior. When the Perfectionist is achieving what they want to achieve then they are on a huge high and once they have achieved what they want then they tend to go to the other end of the spectrum.

A classic example of a Perfectionist is Peter, who trained for the New York marathon. He promised himself once he achieved his goal that he would keep his level of fitness up. It takes a lot of time and energy to achieve the fitness level to run a marathon and unless you are a professional or regular runner it will be hard to maintain this level of fitness. Having a strong Perfectionist trait Peter didn't take this into account and so life began to take over and before he knew it he was back drinking and eating and not going to the gym.

He felt bad about this and the more he felt bad the more he felt down about his ability to stay fit. In fact, what actually happened was the Perfectionist part drove him to run the marathon and once he had achieved this it said, "Well you have achieved this now, you asked me to help you, I did and now it's over." Peter couldn't understand why he had lapsed after being so fit. What Peter didn't realize was that the Inner Critic had stepped in berating him with questions like: "Why are you eating and drinking and not going to the gym?" "What will happen when you won't be ready for the next marathon?" Peter was caught in the vicious and relentless cycle of low self-esteem and lethargy. This was because his Perfectionist part had achieved what it wanted until the same time next year, then his Inner Critic stepped up, berating that he had let his perfection go. Peter lived in this turmoil until the goal of running the New York Marathon once again ignited his Perfectionist.

The Perfectionist is very good at living healthily all week and then suddenly the pressured goal setting to be perfect gives way to anxiety from the expectations you have placed on yourself. This then becomes unadulterated stress. This is when the unconscious mind steps in and asks, "Where can I run away to?" And if your running away tool last time was food, alcohol, excessive exercise or sleeping the day away, then this is what you will use and whatever you use, it will be excessive; over-indulging in food, alcohol or whatever you use to turn off and silence your exhausted Perfectionist.

The Perfectionist part can be so powerful that when it has done its job the mind and body need a complete rest. However, this respite period does not have to be excessive. Rather, this is the time for the Perfectionist to learn new behavior. *The Stress Less Mind* book and CD will help you recognize that you don't have to be perfect all of the time. That it is okay not to be perfect. You will gain an understanding of how to pace your Perfectionist so that it does not hound you into the anxiety stress mode as it has in the past. Through listening regularly to *The Stress Less Mind* CD you will learn to relax, while tuning in and connecting with your Healthy Confident Part. In doing this, your Perfectionist part will begin to understand how to let go and enjoy living life. What a welcome relief!

The Perfectionist Perfects Not Losing Weight

Just to follow on from previously discussing food and weight, the following concept may seem odd to you, but if you are either on a diet or losing weight regularly it simply means your Perfectionist has perfected bingeing and yo-yo dieting. The result is that your unconscious mind thinks this is normal behavior because it equates stress with the anxiety of overeating and bingeing, because it sees things as either black or white, there is no in between. As this happens the Inner Critic steps in and begins to criticize your weight gain and the yo-yo dieting cycle begins. The Perfectionist part equals dieting and the Inner Critic equals overeating, and so the stressful cycle repeats itself year in, year out.

The Perfectionist unconsciously drags up all your past negative experiences and you react emotionally as it says, "Where's the food?" and before you can blink you find yourself raiding the fridge. It is a practice that it has perfected over and over again. This form of overeating has been perfected to such an extent that any conscious recognition of this repetitive behavior will be overridden because the Perfectionist part has you trained to overeat to perfection. Remember, the Perfectionist's job is to make sure you do things one hundred percent perfectly and that is just what it does to perfection.

The Twists and Turns of Life

Being perfect all of the time is not only boring, it can also be unexciting because you can't enjoy the exciting ride that life has to offer. When you live your life through the wisdom of your Healthy Confident Part your intuition increases so you can enjoy the twists and turns of life. What a relief it is to know that being perfect is great but that you don't have to be perfect all the time. When you realize you don't have to be perfect all the time then the pressure is off and both your mind and body synchronize into an inner calmness so you can enjoy achieving with pleasure rather than feeling stressed.

Perfectionists and Depression

If you have a strong Perfectionist part you may suffer from bouts of depression. If you are a high achiever and you cannot accept coming second then this can cause you to drop into depression because you feel you have failed. If you find out you were not accepted by the university you wanted to get into or you did not get the position you tried so hard to get or the relationship that you wanted didn't work out, then these setbacks are guaranteed to lead to an Inner Critic attack. This then leads to the knock-on effect which leads you down into the slippery slope of self-loathing, anger and out of control feelings.

Depression, I believe, is a natural emotional experience which we all go through from time to time, and it is a sign that something is wrong in your life. I am not suggesting that anti-depressants should not be taken, but in many cases depression is the reaction to a situation where there is a strong Perfectionist and/or Inner Critic dialogue going on.

You may be in a situation where you perceive that external people and situations are demanding results from you. If you are critical of yourself because you fear that you may not be able to achieve the expected results, then you may take these demands too seriously and hide behind a strong Perfectionist. This is when you run into the very real danger of placing yourself in the deadly combination of the Perfectionist and the Inner Critic. When these two combine it is a sure-fire way to set yourself up for burnout and then depression.

Failure is simply not an option for a strong Perfectionist personality, so if it does occur the consequences can be frightening, not only for the individual but also the people around them. If you identify with this then it is time to get off the Hamster Stress Wheel and put on *The Stress Less Mind* CD so you can listen and understand that failure is just a word that you don't have to have in your vocabulary when you value yourself.

You will learn as you listen and relax that you can live your life intuitively instead of living your life in the fear of failure. When you let go of the perfect perception you have placed on yourself then you set yourself free and you will discover a life which flows so much better because you will feel emotionally safe.

Your Healthy Confident Part will come to the fore and you will live more intuitively because you have established and strengthened the connection to your positive inner energy. This frees you to be who you want to be rather than who you think you should be, as well as connecting with others more naturally.

You Can't Change Other People

Perfectionists are very good at trying to persuade other people to their way of doing things. They don't like it when people say no when they want them to say yes. Perfectionists can often try to make other people change and that is often why they attract Pleasers into their lives.

My motto is: "You cannot and should not try to change other people in order for you to feel self-fulfilled." Each person is on his or her own life journey. The more you try and ask a person to change, the more unconsciously you are creating anger in this person because they themselves lose the sense of who they are while they are trying to be what you want them to be.

It is important to allow other people to be themselves as you learn to balance the Perfectionist part of yourself. If other people choose to change then that is their freedom of choice. However, if they don't change then there is nothing you can do about it. You need to respect the choices they make as to how they want to live their lives.

It is amazing how a person will naturally change of their own accord as they tire of being bullied by the Perfectionist. Often they change in a way that the Perfectionist does not approve of and this makes the Perfectionist angry. Perfectionists will often continue to coerce someone to change; however, this may make the person they are bullying go in the complete opposite direction. The Perfectionist's continued coercion can force the person to take a stand so they can survive emotionally. When this happens the bullying has backfired leaving the Perfectionist emotionally alone.

The Critical and Judgmental Perfectionist

Perfectionists can be very difficult people to work and live with. I admire people who are both goal driven and Perfectionists because once these people have their mind set to achieve something you know that they will achieve it. This is the up part of the Perfectionist, particularly if it involves something that you know is not your strength. The downside is that, as the Perfectionist tends to suffer bouts of depression they can get snappy. Also, in this down phase they can have heavy negative energy which can sap your positive energy. This can often be a result of jealousy. Jealousy can strike at the Perfectionist, especially when another person achieves what they wanted to achieve, or the jealousy might stem from not having what someone else has when it is something they want.

If the Perfectionist feels they can't achieve what the other person has achieved then they can become critical and judgmental as a way of self-protection. The Perfectionist cannot stand it when someone else is successful at what they want so they will avoid these people. They can appear to be childish because they can sulk with resentment and can be difficult to talk out of this behavior.

The Perfectionist Perfecting Life

The Perfectionist part within you loves to compare you to other people and often seems like the Inner Critic. However, there is a difference, for the Inner Critic is there to protect you by being negative about everything you do, whereas the Perfectionist will only allow you to do things it knows you can do. It will create stress and anxiety within you as a way to protect you from failing.

We are swamped by the media who market various products selling perfection. Beautiful models and actresses who are air-brushed to perfection promote products in the hope that you will buy them. The advertising mindset is that you too will want to have perfect skin, hair or teeth and buy these products.

Advertising billboards all around the world show us perfect people with perfect lives.

One of the most interesting aspects of my work is that it has given me an insight into how people truly think. Everybody assumes that everyone else is having better sex, living healthier lives, having better relationships and are more fulfilled, and yes some people are, but there are also a lot of people who are not. No matter what your Perfectionist thinks – there is not one person who lives the perfect life. Even the wealthy and beautiful people still have to deal with problems that come their way.

Procrastination

Procrastination is one of the strongest signs of the Perfectionist part feeling that it doesn't think it will be able to achieve what it wants to achieve.

The Perfectionist will scan your mind when you want to achieve something and if it can't find any example of success it will tell you, "Don't go there, you will not be successful." The difficulty in this is that even though your unconscious mind and the Perfectionist have decided it is unsafe for you to achieve something, your conscious mind may have a different opinion.

When the conscious mind and the unconscious mind have different opinions the unconscious mind will always win the argument. People often say to me that they don't have any self-control or willpower; however, this is far from the truth. The actual truth is that the Perfectionist part of your unconscious mind deems this new venture as emotionally unsafe and will stop you from achieving the expected outcome.

This is why procrastination sets in. It is not because you are lazy or unsuccessful; it is just that your Perfectionist doesn't see the evidence that you will succeed. Your unconscious mind prevents you achieving what you want to achieve out of fear of failure and looking foolish.

Jim was a person who was very driven in his professional life as an IT consultant. Jim was good at what he did; however, his real passion was painting. He loved doodling while he was at work and often people would comment how clever and talented his doodling was. When people left the company he was always asked to draw the farewell card and he did this with great delight. He was told countless times how if he spent more time being an artist he might be successful at it and actually earn money from it.

Each time Jim heard these complimentary comments his talent stirred lots of stress and anxiety within him. This was his Perfectionist part telling him, "You don't have the information to prove to me that you could be successful so don't go there," and of course most of the time he didn't.

His mother paid for him to go on an artist's retreat where he created beautiful paintings; however, when he came back to the reality of his life the painting urge dried up. His artist part went away and the IT consultant ferociously stepped back in because it was safe.

When Jim came to see me it was so obvious that his Inner Critic, along with his Perfectionist, were holding him back. I said to him that often, when there is severe procrastination, it usually means a strong negative Inner Dialogue. I asked him if he told himself things such as: "You'll never make it as an artist." "Artists are poor." "You're not good enough or talented enough." "People will laugh at you." "You show me success as an artist and then I will allow you to progress."

Jim was shocked that I knew what he was thinking. I said, "No, I do not know what you are thinking, but I do know what underpins your procrastination."

Another Assumed Crystal Ball Moment

I explained to Jim that no-one has a crystal ball to see the future, but what we do know is that if you plan your future with the wisdom and positive energy of your Healthy Confident Part, the part that supports your artistic side, then you will be able to progress and enjoy the journey. Whether you make money out of it or not, if you don't get to the next stage you will never know and you will continue to live with the seething procrastination of what might have been.

Jim started to paint and as he did his self-esteem started to develop and this meant he became happier, less stressed and more the person he longed to be. His stress levels dropped as his Perfectionist and Inner Critic began to recede and his Healthy Confident artistic part stepped forward.

The Stress Less Mind CD in the back of this book is re-educating your mind to tune out past negative beliefs and build resources so that you know you can achieve success without stress and anxiety.

The Perfectionist Suffers in Silence

The Perfectionist will never want to admit to the unobvious things that they haven't achieved to the outside world because they want to stay "perceived" as perfect. They will suffer in silence because their Perfectionist part and their Inner Critic don't want to expose any vulnerability to the outside world. The result is the Perfectionist becoming an emotional, stressed out person. To the outside world they look like they can handle life perfectly, but inside they are a seething, churning, emotional mess just waiting to explode.

I have been helped both personally and professionally through my continued awareness of the wisdom of my Healthy Confident Part, for it is through this part that I reached the realization that no one is perfect and never will be. I often describe examples to clients to demonstrate how powerful the Perfectionist part is so that I can show them that they are not alone, because they do so often feel alone. It also is a reminder to all of us that those who appear perfect have simply perfected this cover as their protective mechanism and that they are far from perfect.

Is This It?

The strange thing is that once Perfectionists achieve their goal that they drove so hard to achieve they can then become despondent because they have nothing to strive for. They question life and ask themselves, "Is this it?" They can feel bored or anxious when there is nothing to achieve and this creates stress. I respect that it is good to have goals; however, the Perfectionist doesn't ever allow you to relax. It makes you feel guilty because it doesn't feel safe when you are just being rather than doing.

The Stress Less Mind book and CD will help you learn how to relax, let go and enjoy the flow of life rather than staying in the stress created by the Perfectionist. Being perfect will become less important as you feel the healing, positive energy of your Healthy Confident Part. As you listen to *The Stress Less Mind* CD you will be de-stressing, so you won't have to achieve perfection all of the time.

When you achieve something, rather than busily searching for the next project you will be able to enjoy the feeling of being in the present of now and not stressing about where you should be.

Perfecting Looking After You

The all or nothing syndrome, as mentioned earlier in this chapter, represents the Perfectionist being absolutely perfect at being good at something or not at all.

The aim for you is to work with your Perfectionist rules so they work with you rather than against any plans you have made. By listening to *The Stress Less Mind* CD you can educate your mind so that you realize that each moment is not about being perfect. It's about having moments where you trust in life rather than pushing and grinding all of the time. When you push you are forcing things to happen which often causes stress and when your goal doesn't go to plan you create more stress and anger within yourself. You become a stress machine.

If your Perfectionist is educated to believe that it is safe for you to have balance, logic, and intuition and that having self-esteem is normal, then it will absorb and perfect this healthy habit rather than being continually driven to either end of the black and white spectrum.

The domino effect of this healthy outlook is that you will experience more peace in your emotional and physical life because you will not be trying to push all the time. Instead you will enjoy living more in the moment.

I am not suggesting that striving for what you want is now out of the equation, rather that while there are times when being number one is good, at other times it's just not going to be possible.

When the Perfectionist works with the Healthy Confident Part, rather than against it, then you will experience more harmony, calmness and wisdom and this will guide you to discover that some moments can be perfect while other moments will be imperfect. And when you discover this then you will realize that the imperfect moments are actually perfect.

The Stress Less Mind book and CD will contribute to your discovery of you and in the process you will notice that you expect less of other people and you are attracting lovely situations into your life. This will affirm that it is safe for you to laugh at yourself more and see the funnier side of life because you won't be taking yourself so seriously. What a pleasure it will be to enjoy each moment rather than constantly being driven to succeed.

Chapter 6

Your Present and Your Future

The Stress Less Mind

Your Present and Your Future

Positive Changes To Your Present Your Future

As you've read through the previous chapters of *The Stress Less Mind* you will have gained insight and understanding into how we are thinking, feeling and learning at all times whether or not we are conscious of it. More importantly, however, you now understand why you are stressed and how you have the ability to change your way of thinking by communicating more effectively with the different parts you have met within *The Stress Less Mind*. And it is with this in mind that we are now going to look at how you can create a more positive life both in the present and the future through connecting with your Healthy Confident Part.

Every moment of your life has been stored in the library of your unconscious mind. And so you have reacted in a particular way in certain situations because you have unconsciously brought these stored memories forward and reacted in the same stressful unwanted behavior patterns.

If your unconscious mind's library has not stored positive information and sensations about feeling less stressed, then it will find and bring forward negative memories and sensations which are detrimental to you and the situation you find yourself in.

Memories are all you have had as your reference library on how you feel and deal with stress, until you read this book! This is one of the most important points to remember consciously. Your stored stress management program in your mind will continue to respond as it always has done until you provide it with new tools. *The Stress Less Mind* CD helps equip you with the tools to change. Listening to *The Stress Less Mind* CD educates the deepest part of your mind so you can recognize that you have a chance to think before you respond negatively, so you can react positively both in the present moment and the future.

This chapter is a reminder about how you can continue to make great progress with your positive Inner Dialogue rather than listening to your negative Inner Critic, because your unconscious mind does have the ability to create new positive healthy responses.

When you train your unconscious mind to tune out negative conversations and tune in to the positive conversations then you can relax, let go and free your mind and body of unwanted stress. Then you can enjoy the pleasure of feeling and hearing the positive healing energy of your Healthy Confident Part. This is, to my knowledge, the fastest and most effective way to become less stressed.

It is the stress that your unconscious mind has created which produces anxiety and fear about life. You may have some serious concerns about situations you face in your present and future life. Or it may be stress about general day-to-day living that plagues you. Either way as you read this chapter you will learn how to combat it so you can get off the Hamster Stress Wheel.

Being in the Present

We all have moments when we think about our past and our future and forget about being in the present. However, stressed-out people live predominantly in either mode instead of living and being in the present. This mind activity in itself is a huge contributor to stress. Living with regrets about your past or panicking about your future is detrimental to your health and it is driven by a strong Inner Critic which is sometimes supported by the Pleaser or the Perfectionist.

Whenever you think about your past or your future negatively you are igniting memories and your mind sends these negative signals to your body and it produces stress chemicals. Then before you know it you are on the road to feeling stressed and fearful about life.

It is normal for us think about the past and the future; however, it can prove to be unhelpful if it makes you feel bad about yourself or angry about what you feel you haven't achieved or feel you can't achieve.

This chapter will help you understand how to think about the past or the future not through the negative eyes of your Inner Critic, but rather through the eyes of the calm energy of your Healthy Confident Part. So that when you do regress into old negative thoughts patterns you will be aware that this is happening and you will have the knowledge and tools to change to a positive and constructive outlook. And when you think about something you would like to achieve in your future you will be able to do this with the constructive wisdom of your Healthy Confident Part. Your Healthy Confident Part is connecting to these positive thoughts and transmitting healing energy throughout your body so you feel less infected by negative thoughts about your past. Moment to moment, day by day, you will feel more confident and relaxed about your future because you will be comfortable being you. Using these healing tools helps you to improve your quality of life and the best part is that all you need to do is enjoy time out to practice. Understanding how to be in the present is a powerful tool to help you enjoy being you right now.

Fear of Being in the Now

A lot of people live focused on the future in the belief that by staying in this state they will always be prepared for the "what if" moments of life. This means they create their own anxiety and fear of what lies ahead in the future. These people live in a permanent state of unnecessary stress because they believe that by being in this future-thinking mode they hold the reins on their life and as a result they will keep on track. They live constantly looking ahead always working on the next project or the next situation to improve their life and consequently they take on too much and can become very stressed out. It is important for these people to realize that while it is good to prepare for the future it is extremely beneficial to take time out to live and enjoy the present.

Being in the present means you can't think about and dwell on the past or the future. *The Stress Less Mind* CD helps you to live and enjoy being in the moment. All you need to do is just take 25 minutes a day, lying or sitting somewhere comfortable and give your mind and body a break from their constant stress. As you do this you will learn to "be" rather than "do" all the time.

This may seem a hard task for many people. However, I can assure you this is one of the most important support mechanisms you will ever learn for it enables you to support yourself emotionally and physically.

As I live a busy life, when I find myself under pressure of time and I have to make a choice between whether to go to the gym or do my self-hypnosis I will always put my hypnosis time first. By doing this I am taking the time to prioritize my emotional mind so I can enjoy being in the present.

Later in this chapter I will talk about how to look positively into your future while listening to *The Stress Less Mind* CD. However, just for now, know that listening to the CD is a wondrous time out to de-stress and pamper yourself and enjoy simply just "being."

Savoring these Moments

There are, of course, many other ways to enjoy taking time out to be in the moment and enjoy life. It may be walking along a beach, climbing a mountain or simply drinking a cup of fresh coffee or savoring a chocolate.

These time out moments are called savoring life when you can enjoy where you are right now. Becoming aware of the choices you make helps you to decide and set into action how to take time out to connect with life in a daily or weekly ritual. Through doing this you will set in motion the inner connection with your intuitive and energetic Healthy Confident Part.

A particular client's savoring time out moment is walking her dog, while for another client it is taking a long luxurious bath. Make a list of all the things you want to savor that will bring you into the present. Doing this will wash away those past fears and anxieties about where you were and allow you to think of the future. Be committed to taking time out for you. I respect that life isn't perfect and there will be times when doing the savoring won't be possible, but don't stress about it because sometimes life throws us little detours. However, regularly doing activities that bring you into the present will give you a great gift. It's called Gratitude. Gratitude is so important in life and I know myself that when I am in the present enjoying the moment of now I feel so humbled and so thankful that I am alive to be me.

When you are busy thinking about and planning your future, life tends to be more about getting to where you are going, so there is less gratitude time to value and enjoy life in the present moment. Constantly worrying about the future is a stressful and futile pursuit because it denies you the experience of connection to the intuitive wisdom of your Healthy Confident Part.

Taking time out to be in the present gives you space in your mind to appreciate your life. You clear away the unnecessary clutter so you can think about the future peacefully and calmly. This simple and accessible tool is really amazing because it actually works!

Each Day is a Separate Day

Changing your emotional and physical relationship with yourself is exciting. As you discover your Healthy Confident Part you will cope better in your daily life and become aware of all the positive examples that surround you.

Your Healthy Confident Part is your savior, for it is this part that will give you a sense of space in your mind and your life so you can enjoy each new day with a more positive attitude. You will learn to think of any difficulties that come your way as challenges or detours that can be circumnavigated, for you will have calmness of mind to think them through. The advantage that your Healthy Confident Part has is that it can prevent one difficult day infecting the next.

How often do you hear yourself or other people say: "I have had such a stressful day, looks like I'm in for a hard week ahead!" Be careful because it can become a self-fulfilling prophecy as you tune in to this negative attitude and tune out the positive. One difficult day does not necessarily make a difficult week. There are times when life situations are beyond your control.

When you see one day as separate from the other days you become free to find each day more enjoyable. You will be giving yourself the opportunity to say to yourself, "Okay, I didn't like what happened but there is nothing I can do about it, so I'll let it go and move on." As soon as you do this, your mind does move on because you are able to let go and move into a healthier space.

When it comes to people losing weight or starting an exercise regime they often find they are in this one day infecting the rest of the week syndrome. With good intentions they make plans to start their healthy eating program or go to the gym on Monday and then Monday comes and they say to themselves, "I'll start next week."

The problem here is that their Inner Critic has kicked in saying such things as: "You are hopeless." "You made a commitment to yourself to lose weight." "You said you would get fit." "You are weak and undisciplined." And so the negative self-berating continues. How stressful is that!

If there is a day when you don't go to the gym then that is absolutely fine. You will notice when listening to *The Stress Less Mind* CD that you can just let go of any of the fears you have about what you have not achieved that day. Remember, you can't change your past or what happened today, so why bother holding on to it. It is a waste of space in your mind and in your life.

At any given time you are thinking thoughts that cause you to feel either good or not so good, in other words you feel either positive or negative. In order to be in alignment with your goal of feeling calmer, safer and more confident about you and your life you need to be aware of your thoughts and how they affect you and those around you. Thoughts can be likened to a magnet, you can either attract positive people and situations into your life or your negativity can cause people to withdraw from you.

Your Emotional Chart

The following landscape chart is an example of a day in the life of one of my clients.

This chart is a great conscious mind tool to see where you may be habitually stressing and why. It will help you to recognize the patterns of how you respond to stress when it may not be necessarily helpful. Use this chart for 30 days: by doing this you will gain great insight into the patterns, the people and the range of emotions that flow through your mind on a daily basis. You will recognize how your unconscious mind can trigger the desire to be irrational and stressed, without you being conscious of it.

If you want to photocopy the emotional chart or re-design it then that is fine. It doesn't matter if you want to reconfigure it or keep it the same. This chart represents understanding what, why, who and when your stress levels go up.

This is not about blaming other people for your stress levels, for your stress levels are your responsibility. However, this chart will show you on a daily basis how much stress is habitual and can most of the time be avoided if you shift your thinking.

If you are feeling stressed, writing it down is incredibly helpful. If you feel very happy, write it down too. All emotions are valid in your understanding of your life. Making note of the good times will enhance your gratitude of life too.

Read through the emotions carefully and see which ones resonate with you the most. You can make a note of them in the chart below. A sample is below for you then a blank page for you to photocopy or re-design to suit you.

- Anger
- Boredom
- Fear
- Anxiety
- Frustration
- Hurt
- Rejection
- Loneliness
- Happiness
- Love

You may also use this chart to look kindly at the people around you who may trigger stressful feelings within you.

Date and Time	Where were you?	Who was with you?	What thoughts triggered you to feel stressed?	What inner Conversations came to your mind that made you feel not good about yourself?	What did you feel like doing?
10th February 3.05pm	Work	My boss	My appraisal review	I was nervous about discussing my appraisal. My boss is a pretty direct person and felt he would criticize me.	Going home sick but know I will just have to face it again tomorrow.
10th February 5pm	After work	My work mate	Discussing the meeting with my boss	Feeling annoyed at having to feel like a child by having an appraisal.	Quitting my job. I don't like being judged. I am having a beer.
10th February 7pm	Home	My wife	Discussing the meeting with my boss. I don't feel safe in my job.	Relieved to be home, the day is over and I can now relax. I am tired.	Eating chocolate but will wait for my evening meal.
11th February	Home	My wife	My wife is trying to make me feel better, however I feel very much alone.	A delicious meal. Feeling safe. Now I am starting to calm down.	Going to bed early to forget my day.
12th February	Home	My wife	I am feeling much more supported at home as my wife and I had a really good conversation.	My Inner Critic is playing games with me. My job is actually safe.	Making love to my wife and we did.

Date and Time	Where were you?	Who was with you?	What thoughts triggered you to feel stressed?	What inner Conversations came to your mind that made you feel not good about yourself?	What did you feel like doing?

Many people have difficult people in their lives and I appreciate that not every person is willing to take responsibility for their own "bad" behavior or the stress they exude which you may pick up on. The point here is that you need to be able to deal with their negativity and not take it on board.

This chart will give you a greater understanding of how much unnecessary stress is in your life because you have created an emotional pattern of thought by absorbing other people's bad behavior and this triggers tension and anxiety within you on a regular basis.

Situational Stress

It is how you interpret the situation that makes it stressful. However, if at this point in time you are going through an unusually stressful period such as separating from a partner or other unusual difficult situations then you are in what I call Situational Stress. These stressful situations are very different from the stress and anxiety you may regularly experience in your daily life.

Bereavement, job loss, a child being ill, all create Situational Stress. *The Stress Less Mind* book and CD will assist you to overcome stress. However, this emotional chart is about seeing on paper right in front of your eyes how often you become stressed, irrational, scared, fearful and negative.

Keep, your chart going for a month. As you do this you will see a pattern emerge of how in the past you have taken on what your unconscious mind perceived as your correct reactive response to any stressful experience. Charting your daily emotional life will give you great insight into your true habitual stress and reactive response pattern and how it does not support you at all. And the exciting thing is you have the ability to change your reactive stress response.

Also, other people and their stressful responses could be affecting you. It could be a difficult boss, a demanding mother, father, or it could be that your child is a challenge. On the other hand, it could be you creating a lot of stress in your place of work or with your partner, children and friends.

I often explain to clients that even though they may not be conscious of it, they may actually enjoy being stressed out or being difficult to be around. They could be the culprit of inducing stress in their lives and stress in the lives of other people who surround them.

There are many people who grew up in an environment where shouting and abusive words were a part of life and they carry this negative stressful behavior pattern forward when they become adults. Or there may have been lots of drama and silent tension in their family home which they carry forward into their relationships. This happens because their unconscious mind absorbed and stored all of this negative behavior at an early age. And even though they originally may have been in fear of these stressful outbursts or intimidation, the unconscious mind gets used to the situation very quickly and it becomes a way of life.

The mind can adapt to anything if it experiences and absorbs it enough. And so you may be the person who is causing stress in yourself and others. Or you may know of someone who actually appears to enjoy having drama in their lives. This is not because they want to be difficult, rather it is a place where they feel the safest.

The unconscious mind, as I have mentioned throughout this book, doesn't know the difference between positive and negative. It just gets used to responses and then assumes these negative responses to be normal. So it is no surprise that if you grew up surrounded by lots of anger and verbal abuse from siblings or bullies at school, or if your parents constantly argued and put each other down and put you down as well, you lived and grew up under constant stress. This then is how you have learned to respond and there is every chance that you brought this negative stressful behavior forward into your current situation.

If you identify with this person then you will actually recognize that you have a lot of drama in your life and you need to respect that up until now this has been your coping strategy. Being in a calm space does not feel safe for you. In fact, it is a foreign place for you to be. People who love drama feel vulnerable when they are in a calm moment because it triggers memories of their past where the calm seemed to always precede the storm.

If you are one of these people then you will be very stuck in focusing on the future, for this is your coping mechanism. And you will be ready to fire off at anybody who may trigger a situation where you feel threatened or scared. You will constantly be on tenterhooks and will not be able to relax because relaxing means you will not be on guard. So you live with lots of unnecessary stress as your coping strategy.

The Stress Less Mind book and CD will help you learn how to disconnect from living in this constant drama state and re-connect with your Healthy Confident Part. It is the Healthy Confident Part that sends the signal to your body to relax and to trust more. So each time you feel a state of drama in your mind and your life is ready to erupt, write it down on your emotional chart.

Jack was a classic "drama queen." He was one fired-up person. When he called to make an appointment with my assistant, she said he was very gruff. He was sent by his boss who said that he needed anger management as he was disturbing the office environment. My assistant warned me and knowing that this behavior is simply a sign of a strong Inner Critic and lots of fear, I was prepared for his attitude.

I knew once we discussed the Inner Critic that he would gain some understanding of how he thought and responded to situations in his life. When I explained to Jack that anxiety and fear were underpinning his anger and that these feelings were his reactive protective mechanism, he really got it.

Jack then went on to tell me that all his life he had felt stressed about being found out. When I asked him what it was that he thought people would find out about him, he replied, "I grew up with a father who had a terrible temper. I was never good enough and in his eyes I was never going to be successful. I dread male authority and in my business I am surrounded by men and I am worried they will see what my father saw. I live in daily fear of what they may be saying about me behind my back. I am always predicting to myself that I will lose my job and now as I am being forced into seeing you, it looks like it will probably happen."

My heart went out to Jack because he had such a strong Inner Critic as well as an external critic – his father. In order for Jack to see that his anger response was in fact an emotionally learned behavior, we needed to bring some positive scenarios into his mind that would allow him to be in the present when he communicated with his colleagues and boss.

These positive scenarios were made up of planning in Jack's mind of being with his colleagues and boss with his Healthy Confident Part present and this would result in healthy endorphins being produced. I suggested to him that whenever he felt any sense of fear to breathe out the Inner Critic voice and all its negative energy and then breathe in and feel the energy of the Healthy Confident Part spreading into every part of his body. This technique is included on the CD, so you too can enjoy training your mind to respond more positively.

Jack diligently listened to his recording and when he came in the next week, he was in much better spirits. He said he felt calmer and not so worried about what other people thought and that even though his Inner Critic still had its strong moments, which is completely natural, the strength of its voice had lessened. Jack now knew the signs of the Inner Critic and how to use his breathing to diminish its negativity.

Using deep, long breaths helps you to feel calm and confident, for they give you some space to respond more appropriately to life and the situations you may find yourself in. When you shallow breathe you keep yourself in an anxious state. Just like Jack, by listening to *The Stress Less Mind* CD, you too will be learning to breathe more deeply as the days and nights go by.

Stopping the Negative Crystal Ball Syndrome

When you plan your future through the eyes of your Inner Critic you will never feel safe, for its job is to make sure you are prepared for the worst case scenario. It will never say to you, "Hey, let's enjoy the ride of life." Whereas when you see your life through your Healthy Confident Part you can enjoy the ride.

You don't have to wait in stressful anticipation of what bad things may happen. What is the point? The only thing this does is to stir up stress and anxiety within you which is completely unnecessary. So let's stop this negative Crystal Ball Syndrome and create some amazing positive moments in your life that represent you feeling good about you and your life.

Planning Your Future in Your Mind

Now we are going to explore one of the most powerful hypnotic techniques in combination with what you have already learned as you read through this book.

Your unconscious mind can create anything if you give it enough space and time, and reading through the following pages as well as listening to *The Stress Less Mind* CD supports these techniques.

Fortunately, there is now scientific evidence that our thoughts can influence and create reality, either positive or negative. And it has been agreed that hypnosis or meditation is the quickest, safest and most effective way to create emotional and physical changes.

When you use the crystal ball to create a perception in your unconscious mind of what you think your future looks like and you predict it to be negative or fearful then your mind and body produces negative energy because it assumes that this is what is going to happen. And then you find that you are continually stressed and troubled because your unconscious mind has trained itself to think this is the natural outcome.

As your unconscious mind doesn't know the difference between imagination and reality, when you project your future thoughts positively it actually thinks and prepares for the good times. Your mind is actually happy and relieved to experience good times. And if you give your unconscious mind enough time and attention to think and absorb pleasant, positive thoughts, just as you do for negative thoughts and feelings, then it will assume these positive thoughts to be true too.

You may recall times when you have been in the daydream state where you have thought about your future without any conscious effort. During this time you may have imagined what it would feel like to pass an exam or find that new relationship you desire. It could be daydreaming about that new job or feeling safe within yourself as you cope well with difficult situations. It doesn't matter what the images are, what is important is how you feel about these positive images you have created.

There have been many books recently that suggest that you can create a positive future just with your thoughts and to a certain extent this is true. However, it can only be true if your feelings are the same as the images you create in your mind. Your thoughts and feelings must match or else your mind will revert to your old, negative ways.

If you imagine being assertive with a difficult person in your life but you feel fear at the same time, you are placing yourself in internal conflict. Your mind assumes that this is a vulnerable situation and will not allow you to go there. Whereas if your mind and body are in positive agreement then it feels that it is safe for you to be more assertive and it will be more than happy for you to go there in the reality of your life.

Hypnosis is the easiest and most effective way to do this, for it connects your mind and body to feel and be safe in the given situation you find yourself in and you let go of your stress triggers. When you imagine in your mind to think the opposite of negative and think positively, then you create positive responses and your unconscious mind will learn very quickly that this is how you respond.

If you want to feel less stressed, then your mind and body need to have supporting knowledge of how to feel safe to let these sensations go. Otherwise it is virtually impossible to let go. I believe that if you want to feel better in yourself then your mind and body need to communicate with each other on the same level so they respond by connecting positively to each other, confirming that it is safe for you to feel safe.

Margaret's Story

Margaret came to see me after having tried a lot of different therapies to deal with her anxieties. She was reticent about seeing me as she was nervous about hypnosis; however, she was also desperate to change her emotional state.

Margaret had a lot of fears about her life. She was a terrible sleeper, had regular panic attacks and suffered with Irritable Bowel Syndrome. Margaret was a born worrier which had created a lot stress in her emotional and physical life.

In Britain there are now some hospitals that are using hypnosis to deal with Irritable Bowel Syndrome which is a condition where the digestive tract spasms causing urgent bowel movements often at inappropriate times. It can be very stressful for the person who has IBS because they can become a prisoner of their own body, planning their meal times and activities to avoid any rush to the toilet.

It was clear that Margaret's anxieties about life were manifesting physically in her body and that hypnosis would be the perfect tool to support her to feel well and in control of her body again.

When I asked Margaret what worried her she replied, "We lost a lot of money in the recession in 2008 which has put a lot of pressure on my husband and me and on our earning capacity. I worry a lot about my family and in particular about one of my sons who is 18. He doesn't cope very well with life and doesn't seem to know what to do with his life. My husband and he clash all the time because he wants my son to get out and get a job. I am constantly trying to keep the peace at home. I worry about his financial future as well as ours. It's a constant state of stress in our house with no foreseeable reprieve."

Margaret's stresses were real; however, worrying about them constantly was creating more stress and this was causing Margaret to be physically unwell.

When I asked Margaret how she saw her future she went into instant panic mode. Her body language said it all. She became tense and closed up. Margaret's mind together with her Inner Critic had been predicting the worst case scenarios of the house being repossessed, her son living with them for the rest of their lives, along with an angry husband who couldn't relate to his own son.

So it was no surprise to learn that at that present moment in time any thoughts about the future were unhelpful to Margaret because her unconscious mind had connected the future with fear, uncertainty and potential financial ruin.

Throughout this book I have been talking about how the unconscious mind learns very quickly to try and avoid feeling vulnerable, and in Margaret's mind thinking about the future meant she was prepared for the worst. This is the irony, once the mind plays these moments in an attempt to forewarn us, it makes the situation seem out of control and unmanageable.

In Margaret's case we needed to do some serious Inner Critic work. Margaret also had a strong Pleaser personality which was exacerbating the IBS. Margaret's Pleaser was trying to resolve everybody else's problems, but alas this was not possible.

Margaret's mind had connected thoughts of the future with fear, anxiety and a sense of hopelessness and this was then triggering an inter-connection of feelings in her body and particularly her digestive system.

I wanted Margaret to know that her mind was thinking about her future too much and trying to resolve too many external situations that she could not change. So the first hypnosis session was to educate Margaret's unconscious mind to tune into her Healthy Confident Part so her body would produce helpful, healthy endorphins in her digestive system. We worked with her breathing to train her to breathe to a much deeper level. We did this so that each time she felt overwhelmed with fear she would know how to breathe the fear out. Through breathing deeply she felt calm.

As Margaret had connected the future with fear and anxiety, we rehearsed in her mind over and over again this breathing technique. This coupled with a recording I made for her, she learned to trust in her future by just taking one day at a time.

Margaret came in to see me the next week and was amazed at how much calmer she felt. Her IBS had improved, but more importantly she was less worried about the future.

Margaret's story is one of many where a person's mind has played games with them and held them back from trusting in their future. This is the reaction of the unconscious mind where all the emotional habits are stored. If you see your future negatively over a period of time then the unconscious mind will assume that this is the reality and it will support these thoughts with responding physical sensations of stress chemicals. With Margaret, it was not that these feelings were correct, but rather a learned habitual response that could be changed.

Planning Your Positive Future

If you have a fear of the future it is a learned behavior that can be changed. It is not the truth but an opinion of what may happen. *The Stress Less Mind* book is a powerful tool to help re-educate your mind so you can learn that your negative response is actually not right or healthy for you, rather your stress response is what your Inner Critic thinks is appropriate.

For you to feel less stressed about your future, you need to travel there in your mind first so you can re-program your opinions about your future.

As your mind doesn't know the difference between reality and imagination you can train it to see and feel the future with optimism, clarity and confidence.

Remember, hypnosis is like attending school in the inner world of your mind where you can learn a new language of how to feel good in yourself no matter what turbulence is going on in your life.

If there is anything that is causing you to feel stressed about your future, to my knowledge the quickest and most effective way to adjust to feeling calm is for you to experience self-hypnosis.

Your Future Technique

So now all you need to know and do is just simply lie or sit somewhere safe and warm where you can relax and listen to *The Stress Less Mind* CD and begin to train your mind to de-stress. Perhaps at times you could also listen to some relaxing music that soothes you or you can be just in a quiet space to reflect on gratitude and inner calmness.

Now as you do this, bring forward in your mind a stressful moment that is occurring in your life right now. No matter what the situation is or whether it can be resolved at this present time or not, just practice imagining yourself feeling calm. Take a deep breath in and release any tension or anxiety as you breathe out. Now I want you to go to the end of the stressful situation and see it as being resolved (even if you can't imagine it being resolved). See yourself feeling free from the situation. See yourself having a positive conversation with yourself. See yourself coping with all the people who are involved with more confidently whether these people are difficult or not. See yourself being assertive and saying what you want to say so that your voice is being heard. Keep creating and playing positive scenarios in your mind.

As you now know, the mind sees things as real, so the more you create and play with these imagined scenarios in your mind then the more it thinks they are real. The amazing domino effect is that your body will respond to your mind by producing healthy, calming endorphins. Keep doing this if you can each day.

Although it may seem too simple to be true, this is the best way to train your mind to relax so you can trust yourself in all situations that may or may not happen in your life. You have an amazing mind that once given the opportunity to see how expansive your positive thoughts can be, the more it will assume this is how to respond to your life.

Staying On Track with Your Goals

There are so many different situations where through using this technique you will be more able to stay on track with your goal of feeling well emotionally and physically. If there is any situation where you feel stressed, remember that your mind can learn how to see whether the glass is half full or half empty. You will have the ability to trust and let go of fear so that you will hold the view that everything will be okay because you have shown your unconscious mind first that it will be.

There are times when things don't go to plan, but when that happens if you trust your Healthy Confident Part you can re-adjust because you are aware that this means something better is about to come along. You need to trust that these situations are just the wonderful twists and turns of life.

Of all of the hypnosis techniques this future one is my favorite as it lifts the spirits of clients on every level because it shows them that their mind is creative and imaginative. When you plan in your mind seeing and feeling positive outcomes then this is the quickest and fastest way to show your unconscious mind that this is how life is – calm, more trusting, more optimistic and positive.

Whenever I am in fear of the future, I take myself either to my bed, couch or some place where I can relax and see the outcome in my mind with lots of fun, love and happiness. I know that if the situation doesn't turn out that way then something better is coming, because I know that my mind is in full swing to embrace a safe and positive future as this is what I believe to be true.

Sometimes I get caught up in the crossfire of life situations and question why? And when this happens I remind myself that it just means something more amazing is going to happen that will enhance my life.

This is what I help people to do, I help them to instill in their own minds a sense of unique trust, a trust that comes when they live their lives with the wisdom of their Healthy Confident Part rather than their Inner Critic. For life is very rarely perfect, and I like this fact because it means there is an abundance of opportunities that can come your way. When you are open to the wonders of life rather than shutting yourself down you are open to the belief that all things can happen, and through thinking this way you can turn your life around.

It's not the life that matters, it's the courage that you bring to it.
(Harbhajan Singh Khalsa Yogiji) Yogi Bhajan

This quote says it all for me. For having courage to create changes in your life is the biggest gift you can give to yourself. For without courage nobody would make progress in their lives.

The Stress Less Mind book is a big step to help you see within yourself that you have the courage to change your thinking and improve your relationship with yourself. The courage to see that you are worthy as a person, the courage to feel positively in charge of your life rather than living through the negative eyes of your Inner Critic. This is the greatest gift you can give to yourself.

Stress is fear and fear inhibits courage; however, with the help of *The Stress Less Mind* CD you will notice that each time you listen to the CD you will feel more courageous. You will feel bolder, wiser, calmer and clearer about your life because you will see for yourself that you have an amazing mind that can support you emotionally and physically irrespective of your past.

Your Mind Holds the Key

Whether it is fear of flying, going for that interview or simply feeling better about your life, your mind holds the key. There is no secret to being a calm and more confident person, it is just a learned behavior.

When you plan your future in hypnosis with the wisdom of your Healthy Confident Part you are effectively planning and connecting your mind and body energetically on the deep cellular level. This leads to a life better than your conscious mind can bring you. Every part of your mind and body is tuned into these wonderful sensations. So anytime you feel frightened, scared, stressed or anxious take five minutes out of your day to breathe deeply and release the stress, or listen to *The Stress Less Mind* CD and imagine the stressful situation feeling and being better. Using all of your senses, hear what is going on positively, notice what you are wearing and what makes you feel calm, hear your own voice saying assertively what you want to say. Keep creating and bringing in many different scenarios in your mind that reflect a positive outcome.

This future technique is so powerful that once you start to do it regularly you will notice that it is not just the stressful situation in your life that is improving, but that there is a positive domino effect on other areas of your life.

You will notice that everything is easier to deal with, including those difficult people in your life. You will notice that your life flows much better because you are managing your life through the eyes of your Healthy Confident Part that acknowledges that feeling safe is a normal sensation rather than fearful feelings. You will see for yourself that you are in control of your destiny in a positive way and that you have choices, rather than listening to your Inner Critic and its negative predictions of what "might be."

The Stress Less Mind book and CD is your stress management tool. You will never not have stress in your life, which is why I called the book *The Stress Less Mind*, the difference is in how you manage your stress. Remember, you are learning to manage it rather than letting it manage you, and this is the biggest and most rewarding aspect of training your mind. To have and know that the positive Inner Dialogue you are creating is real and it is effective and becoming more natural to you.

The top tip is to keep listening to *The Stress Less Mind* CD as much as you can. Just 25 minutes a day is all you need and if you can't manage it everyday then that is fine, just don't stress yourself about it. A couple of times a week is good, although you will probably enjoy taking this opportunity to relax and take time out from your everyday life.

Hypnosis is an amazing tool which can be used where or when you want to experience positive change. So anytime you want to improve the quality of your thoughts re-read *The Stress Less Mind* and take 25 minutes to create the outcome in your mind first. Remember, the mind thinks it is real and it will create the best and most positive outcome. Your mind just needs the practice!

Enjoy learning to believe in yourself and your ability to cope with whatever comes your way through the wisdom of your Healthy Confident Part. As you connect your mind and body energetically you will adapt to the abundance which will come your way. All you need to do is relax, let go of stress and welcome all the positives that life has to offer.

Bibliography

The Stress Less Mind

Bibliography

Further Reading and Resources

Georgia Foster can be contacted via her website:
www.georgiafoster.com or telephone UK local call rate
0845 660 4396. Internationally +44 208 987 2718

Suzy Greaves, The Big Peace, Finding Yourself Without Going Anywhere, Hay House (2009)

Voice Dialogue books:
Stone, Hal and Sidra. Embracing Our Selves, Nataraj Publishing, 1989
Stone, Hal and Sidra. Embracing the Inner Critic, HarperSanFrancisco, 1993

David. Hamilton, Ph.D, How Your Mind Can Heal Your Body, Hay House Publishing (2008)

UK Press Office
SUE BLAKE MEDIA RELATIONS
www.sueblakemedia.co.uk

Australian Press Office
DI ROLLE
www.dirolle.com

USA Press Office
STELLAR COMMUNICATIONS
www.e-pr.com